PASSAGES™

Draven's Defiance

Paul McCusker

Tommy™
NELSON

Thomas Nelson Inc.
Nashville

DRAVEN'S DEFIANCE
Copyright © 2000 by Focus on the Family. All rights
reserved. International copyright secured.

Library of Congress Cataloging-in-Publication Data requested.

ISBN 1-56179-844-4

A Focus on the Family book published in Nashville,
Tennessee, by Tommy Nelson™, a division of Thomas
Nelson, Inc.

The author is represented by the literary agency of Alive
Communications, 1465 Kelly Johnson Blvd., Suite 320,
Colorado Springs, CO 80920.

This is a work of fiction, and any resemblance between the
characters in this book and real persons is coincidental.

Editor: Larry K. Weeden
Front cover design: Peak Creative Group

Printed in the United States of America

00 01 02 03 04 QPV 10 9 8 7 6 5 4 3 2 1

A Note to Parents
from Focus on the Family

Adventures in Odyssey's "Passages" series has been designed to retell Bible stories in such a new and creative way that young readers will be able to experience them as if for the first time.

All the "Passages" novels are based squarely on key episodes of scriptural history. Anyone who is intimately acquainted with the Bible will recognize the basic outlines and spiritual lessons of the stories. But the names have been changed, the details have been altered, and (most importantly) the settings have been shifted to the land of *Marus*—an exciting world accidentally "discovered" by a group of kids from Odyssey.

Why this fictional device? Because familiarity can dull the impact of an oft-told tale. By "dressing up" the biblical stories in a new set of "clothes," we hope to release their inherent power in new ways ... and change young lives in the process.

This strategy didn't originate with "Passages." C.S. Lewis did exactly the same thing when he wrote *The Chronicles of Narnia*. Narnia was born when Lewis came to the realization that fantasy can be a particularly powerful tool for communicating gospel truths. "By casting all these things into an imaginary world," he once wrote, "stripping them of their stained-glass and Sunday School associations, one could make them for the first time appear in their real potency" (from Lewis's essay "Sometimes Fairy Stories May Say Best What's to Be Said"). This is exactly what we are trying to do with "Passages."

Parents should also be aware that, consistent with similar elements in the biblical accounts, these books contain occasional scenes of supernatural activity.

As has always been the case with *Adventures in Odyssey*, we sincerely hope that parents and children will read and discuss the "Passages" novels *together.* That's the best way to avoid misunderstanding.

for Dale, with love

Adventures in Odyssey Presents
Passages, Book V

PROLOGUE

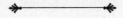

The old man sat in a plastic lawn chair next to the empty fountain. Stone angels watched silently over a stone sea monster that should have been spitting water into the air. Matted leaves collected around the clawed feet of the leviathan.

It was only a little after 10 in the morning, and the air was crisp and clean. The old man, bundled up in a heavy overcoat, lifted his face to the warm sun. Sunglasses perched on his wrinkled nose. Thin strands of white hair fell across the lenses, and he brushed them away as if he still had a full head of hair. His chapped lips were turned up in a practiced smile. Tucked under his chin was a scarf, knotted by his own hand. He looked for all the world like an eccentric college professor.

John Avery Whittaker, or Whit as he was best known, and his good friend Jack Allen watched the old man. They had met him only a few minutes before, and after an exchange of hellos and some idle talk about the weather, they had sat down on the patio behind the sprawling mansion called Hillingdale Haven. That's where their conversation now took an unexpected turn. The old man wanted to tell them about this place that had become his home.

"Hillingdale Haven is an architect's nightmare," the old man said, hooking a thumb toward the building behind them. "It's a pompous mansion built with all the excessiveness of the Victorians. Just look at the size of those red stones! They were imported all the way from Colorado, I understand. It's so ugly that it's beautiful." The old man stopped to cough. He sipped some water through a straw from a plastic cup.

Whit and Jack glanced back at the building. The old man was right. The mansion looked overblown somehow, as if whoever built it were trying to prove something to someone. But Whit and Jack hadn't come out from Odyssey to hear a lecture about the rest home where the old man lived. They had come to ask him about the Marus Chronicles, the four notebooks they'd read over the past few days about a parallel world that kids from Odyssey said they had visited. This was James Curtis, after all, the mysterious author of the manuscripts. And if what he'd written was to be believed, he had been to Marus himself. But the two men thought it would be better to let him talk at his own pace for a while before they bombarded him with all the questions they wanted to ask. They had to be patient, they knew. They didn't want to offend him.

James Curtis continued his lecture. "Hillingdale Haven was built in 1897 and '98 by the railway tycoon Harold Hillingdale. At the time, it boasted several enormous rooms on the ground floor that served as reception and dining halls, a library, a study, a pool and billiards room, a play room for the children, and an assortment of other rooms with no stated purpose. The second floor contained 27 bedrooms of various sizes and shapes. The servants slept in another seven bedrooms tucked away in the attic on the third floor." He suddenly asked, "Did you look around when you came in?"

Whit shook his head. "The receptionist brought us straight out to you," he replied. Then he added, "I've been here before."

"Oh, yeah, the wife of your friend is here," James acknowledged. "Tom Riley's wife, Agnes. We talk sometimes. She's a sweet woman."

Whit nodded. Tom Riley's wife lived at Hillingdale Haven because she suffered from depression. It often left her unable to do even the most basic functions, so she and Tom had agreed that she'd be better off with professional care. Hillingdale Haven became her home.

James stared at the fountain. "Hillingdale Haven was Harold Hillingdale's 'country home,' you see. It's where he brought his family to escape from the rigors of life in the big city of Cincinnati." James smiled. "It was also convenient that Hillingdale owned the train line from Cincinnati to Connellsville, with a stop in Odyssey. That made it easy to get his family here. Then Hillingdale died in 1924, and his family decided to get rid of the mansion. It was sold to a firm that thought the mansion was the perfect place for a sanatorium.

"I remember sneaking onto the grounds as a boy, looking at the people as they walked around, hoping to catch a glimpse of someone barking at the moon or wearing a straitjacket. Then I learned that it wasn't an asylum for the insane but a place for those suffering from specific diseases and nonthreatening mental illnesses to rest and recover. When I was young, I often wondered what it was like for people to be so old that they couldn't live in normal houses." The old man paused for a moment, his face filled with sadness. "And now here I am."

Whit and Jack exchanged glances. They both wondered at that moment if James Curtis was at Hillingdale Haven because he'd grown old or because he suffered from a mental illness.

James sighed. "The ensuing years brought many changes to the mansion as new wings with more rooms were added to the sides and the back. That's how they can fit so many of us in here. It's a nice place, I think. I'm comfortable. But I don't expect to be here much longer."

"Are you going somewhere?" Jack asked.

James smiled. "If my prayers are answered, I'll go back to Marus."

That was Whit's cue. "May we talk to you about Marus now?" he inquired.

"Of course," James answered. "I know you didn't come to hear me jabber about Hillingdale Haven. I only gave you that little history lesson so you'll know my brain is working all right. I'm not a senile old man. I pay attention to my world. I know where I am. Ask me anything you want."

Whit and Jack looked at each other and suddenly laughed. Now that they had the chance, neither knew where to start.

"I'll tell you what," James offered. "How about if I tell you how I wound up here?"

"That's a good place to start," Whit agreed.

"Well, you know from the story about Glennall that I went to Marus. After I came back to Odyssey, I took my 'call' from the Unseen One very seriously. You see, I didn't think I'd been given gifts to use for Marus alone. I figured the Unseen One—God—wanted me to use my gifts and talents in *this* world as well."

"You thought you'd continue to have dreams in this world as you did there?" Jack asked.

"I didn't know. I thought I might, but I never did." James shrugged, then said, "But that didn't matter. I thought that, in time, God would help me understand what He wanted me to do for Him. So I threw myself into studying at school and going to church. That's how I met Maude McCutcheon. She taught English and was my Sunday school teacher, too. One day in school, she asked us to write a story about anywhere we'd ever been or would like to be. I wrote about Marus. It was the first time I did."

Whit asked, "You didn't tell anyone about Marus before? Not even your Aunt Edna?"

"Nope," replied James. "When I came back, I had a feeling deep in my gut that no one would believe me. Or they'd think I was crazy and lock me up. So I decided to keep it to myself." He looked thoughtful. "I sometimes wonder why I took the chance to write about it. I think I trusted Maude McCutcheon. She was a good teacher. I never believed she would laugh at me."

"So what happened?" Jack inquired.

James chuckled as he remembered. "Oh, you should have seen the expression on her face when she walked into class the next day! Her eyes were wide, and she looked excited about something. She asked me to stay after school. Then, when all the other students had gone home, she told me she thought I was a gifted writer. She said my paper about Marus made it seem real to her. Then she asked if it *was* real."

"Did you tell her?" Whit asked.

"Yes. Like I said, I trusted her. And then she pulled out an old diary of her own that told all about *her* adventure in Marus."

"You must've been surprised," Jack observed.

"You could've knocked me over with a feather," James acknowledged with a nod. "It never occurred to me that I'd meet someone else who'd been to Marus. So we compared notes. She'd been there years and years *after* my adventure, even though she'd gone years *before* I did."

"Our time and Marus time don't line up," Whit suggested.

"They sure don't. Which makes things a little confusing

when you're trying to write it all down."

"Why *did* you write it down?" Jack asked.

"To keep a record, of course. And because she thought I was a good writer, Mrs. McCutcheon made me the official chronicler. I was honored. She even let me rewrite her story from her diary so I could fill in a few of the missing pieces about her family and where she'd come from. She wanted them to be consistent, told with my writing style. But for a long time, it was just our stories."

"How did you find out about the others?" Whit asked.

"Through Mrs. McCutcheon. You see, after I grew up here, I went on to college in Boston, then to seminary because I felt God wanted me to be a pastor. One thing led to another, and I eventually became a missionary to English- and French-speaking countries in Europe and Africa. I served as a chaplain in World War II and even spent time in a German prisoner-of-war camp. Over the years, whenever I returned to Odyssey to visit my Aunt Edna, I also spent time with Mrs. McCutcheon. Again, to my surprise, she had found someone else who'd been to Marus."

"Wade Mullens?" Jack asked.

"Yeah. Wade was one of her students."

"What about Kyle and Anna?" Jack wondered. "They weren't students. According to your story, they didn't live in Odyssey at all."

James accepted the comment with a nod. "They visited their grandparents that summer. Which is how Mrs.

McCutcheon learned about their adventure. Their grandparents went to her church."

Just then a woman dressed in a pale-blue dress arrived with a tray of hot drinks. She gave Whit and Jack cups of coffee. James had some hot cocoa. After making sure they were comfortable and James wasn't too cold, she went off.

Whit started their conversation again by asking, "Are there more stories?"

James nodded. "I have a few more manuscripts here with me. Other manuscripts were sent around to other believers for safekeeping."

"Like Wade's mother?" Jack suggested.

"That's right."

"You have all the stories about Marus?" Whit asked.

"No. I've chronicled some, but there are others I haven't had time to do. And I suspect there are some we don't even know about."

A pause followed as Whit and Jack sipped their coffee. It was hard to take it all in. James sounded sane and spoke of Marus as casually as other people might talk about any town or country they'd visited. And yet …

Whit wasn't sure what to ask next, so he returned to James's story. "How did you wind up at Hillingdale Haven?"

"I had to retire from my missions work. A couple of know-it-all doctors said I was getting too old. They said I was showing the early symptoms of Alzheimer's disease." He snorted as he said the last phrase.

Whit looked concerned. "I'm sorry," he said sympathetically.

"Don't be," James said quickly. "They're wrong. They only said that because I'd been a little loose-tongued about Marus and they thought I was crazy." He harrumphed. "I made the mistake of saying that I hoped the Unseen One would some-how allow me to return to Marus before I died. It was always home to me after I'd been there, and I'd still like to go back. It was a heartfelt wish that I was foolish enough to say out loud to the wrong person."

"Do you still think you'll go back?" Whit asked.

"I hope so."

There was another pause as they enjoyed their drinks.

Jack spoke next, an uncharacteristic edge to his voice. "So, Mr. Curtis, let me get this straight," he began. "You're telling us that these stories about Marus are real? They actually happened?"

James looked surprised by the question. "That's exactly what I'm telling you."

"And you expect us to believe that?" Jack asked.

"Why wouldn't you?"

"First, because you've written stories about another *world*."

"So? Can either of you assure me beyond a shadow of a doubt that other worlds don't exist? Where does it say that God hasn't created other worlds?"

Whit considered all the arguments he'd heard on the subject of parallel worlds, other universes, and wormholes through space. Some people believed in them; some didn't. But Whit had to concede that no one could say beyond a shadow of a doubt that other worlds didn't exist. "That's a fair point," Whit finally agreed.

Jack wasn't finished yet. "Second, the world you write about very coincidentally mirrors our own—and contains events that are almost identical to the Bible events that have happened in *this* world."

"What about them?" James replied nonchalantly as he took a drink of his cocoa. The steam touched his sunglasses with silver spray.

Jack looked puzzled. "Doesn't that seem odd to you? I admit it's a clever idea. It's the kind of thing Whit would do at Whit's End to help the kids understand the Bible better. But why would God do that for real?"

"How can I answer a question like that?" James replied in exasperation. "Why did God create *this* world? Why does God do anything at all? I can't answer such a question." James looked at them carefully, his brow furrowed. "You don't believe in Marus, do you?"

Whit and Jack were speechless. The question had been posed to them before, and they didn't know how to answer. The possibility of it was certainly worth exploring—it was an intriguing idea—but did either of them truly believe in it?

Finally Whit said, "We don't know what we believe, Mr. Curtis. We're still trying to figure it out. That's why we wanted to meet you and ask you about it."

"I'm not afraid of your questions," James said defiantly. "But I won't make up answers just to convince you about Marus."

"But you have to admit that it's all pretty far-fetched," said Jack.

"As a Christian, I believe in a lot of things that some people consider far-fetched." James's jaw was set, and Whit knew there would be little sense in arguing with him.

Jack wasn't ready to give up, however. "But consider it from an objective point of view," he continued. "You wrote all the manuscripts. It would've been easy for you to take the Bible stories, adapt them to Marus, and then throw in some real kids from Odyssey just to give them some zing. Right? Come to think of it, you didn't even write your own adventure in the first person."

"I'm a chronicler, not an autobiographer," James stated. "The writers of the Gospels didn't always write 'we' or 'I.' Besides, I didn't say I wrote all the stories."

"What do you mean?" Whit asked.

"There are a few stories I know about but never got the full accounts from the people involved. And there's one written by someone else."

"Someone else?" Jack inquired. "Who?"

"Have you ever heard of Scott Graham?" he asked.

Jack had to confess that he hadn't.

Whit frowned in concentration and tugged at his white mustache. "I remember something about Scott Graham. Is he the one who disappeared from Odyssey back in the '70s?"

"In the summer of 1979."

"I wasn't here then," Jack admitted.

"It was a big case," Whit explained. "Scott Graham had gone down to the railroad tracks with some friends. They were train buffs and wanted to see a new type of train that was supposed to come past Odyssey. Then Scott simply disappeared."

"What do you mean, *disappeared?*" Jack asked skeptically.

"If I remember right, he'd gone into a train tunnel in full view of his friends and never came out again."

"He must've gone out the other side."

"Not according to the railway worker who was testing a signal over there."

"Then he fell into a hole. An underground mine shaft. A sinkhole."

"It was checked thoroughly again and again by the police, then by experts," Whit said. "They couldn't find any reason for his disappearance. He was never found."

Jack turned to James. "And you're going to tell us he disappeared to Marus," he challenged.

James smiled and shrugged.

Jack thought about it a moment, then said, "How could you know if he never came back to *this* world?"

"Because I have the manuscript telling about his adventure."

"Ah," Jack replied quickly, "but how could he tell you about his adventure if he never came back?"

"He didn't tell it to me. He wrote it himself."

"What?" Jack exclaimed.

Whit nearly dropped his coffee mug. "He wrote it himself?" he repeated.

With great effort, James got out of his chair. "Come to my room," he said.

James Curtis lived in one of the original bedrooms of Hillingdale Haven. That meant his room had far more character than the more-institutional rooms built later. He got to enjoy a small fireplace along one of the walls; two large, wood-framed windows; a sink in one corner; and ornate woodworking along the ceiling and around the door itself. He slept in a four-poster bed, worked at an antique writing table, and occasionally sat in a wing chair and watched a small television attached to the wall. Whit noticed a collection of local, national, and international newspapers scattered on a round coffee table. Other books were scattered around the room as well, a few best-sellers but mostly classic titles of prayer and meditation. Thomas à Kempis's *Imitation of Christ* caught Whit's eye.

From a dresser drawer, James produced a handwritten manuscript. Unlike the other Marus manuscripts Whit and Jack had seen, this one wasn't written in an old-fashioned school notebook. It was a photocopy of a manuscript that had been scrawled on plain, lined paper. The pages were held together by a rubber band.

"The handwriting is not mine," James pointed out as he handed the bundle to Whit.

It certainly wasn't James's handwriting—Whit could tell that right away. And, unlike the others, it didn't have a title or a date written near the top. "By the way," Whit had to ask, "what did the dates in your manuscripts mean?"

"Those dates were when the story first happened or was first chronicled," James replied. "They don't mean much to anyone except me." He gestured to the wing chair and then pulled out his desk chair. "Please make yourselves at home while you read."

Jack tilted his head a little, glancing down at the papers. "So this is the story of a boy who disappeared into a railway tunnel," he observed.

"That's right," James answered. "I'm sure you'll have questions when you've finished."

Whit knew they would.

CHAPTER ONE

Ouch was the first thing I thought when I opened my eyes and looked around the dark railway tunnel. I lifted my hand to my forehead. I felt a bump but no blood. I struggled to sit up.

Ouch. My hands scraped against the gravel under me. Whoever designed these railway tunnels didn't build them for pedestrians, that's for sure. I looked up and saw the thing that had knocked me flat. It was a short beam with an iron ring attached. I knew it was a leftover from the old days, when the railway workers hung lanterns in the tunnels.

I felt embarrassed. I should have remembered it was there. But when I had started to run through the tunnel, my eyes were dazzled from the afternoon sunlight and didn't adjust to the dark in time. I hadn't thought to look for anything hanging down like that. So *kaboom*, I banged my head on it.

The smell of oil and soot made my nose twitch, and I held back a sneeze. The railway tunnel stretched out in both directions from where I sat. With a little catch in my breath, I realized something was wrong. It was darker outside than it had been a minute ago—darker than when I first went into the tunnel. It had been a clear summer's day, not a cloud in sight, so the sun couldn't have faded that way.

And where were Donny and Mike? They were my two friends who had come with me to the railroad tracks to see the new Chicago-to-Dallas *Turbo-Fire* train engine. I remembered, too, that I was going through the tunnel to talk to some man on the other side who was working near the tracks. We thought he might know exactly when the train was coming.

Scrambling to my feet, I decided to go back to where Donny and Mike were waiting when I went into the tunnel. They'd been sitting on the bank next to the tracks. It was our favorite spot because it overlooked an older section of the tracks where the trains had to slow down for the bend into the tunnel. "Hey!" I shouted as I jogged to the end of the tunnel. "Mike! Donny!"

I came out into the sunlight and right away started to worry. Mike and Donny weren't there. And the sun was definitely lower in the sky, as if it were just about to go down. I put my hands on my hips and looked around. How long was I knocked out? I figured it was only a minute, maybe not even that long. But it must've been longer. Did Mike and Donny run for help because they thought I was hurt? But why would both of them go? Why didn't one of them stay with me? Or they could have gotten that railway man to help. I mean, they wouldn't just leave me lying there.

Or would they?

Boy, did I have a few choice words for them.

"Mike! Donny! Quit fooling around!" I shouted just in case they were playing a trick. Yelling made my head hurt, though. I lightly touched my bump.

Ouch.

I made my way up the bank and knew right away that something else was different. When Mike, Donny, and I had sat on the bank before, the grass had been green. I had thought about how damp it was because of the rain we'd had the day before. But this grass was dry and brittle. I shrugged and carried on. At the top of the bank, I could see the bridge that formed the top of the tunnel. Beyond that we'd seen the railway worker messing around with a signal by the tracks. That's why I'd run into the tunnel in the first place. Now, though the tracks shot out as far as I could see, there was no railway man.

I sat down, still feeling a little woozy, and tried to think things through. Everything looked awfully strange. Even though it was dusk, all the colors seemed brighter than usual. The brown grass looked golden. The gray gravel along the railroad tracks seemed like a bright gray. The red brick of the tunnel leaped out at my eyes. Even the black lines of the tracks themselves looked sharp, as if somebody with a fine-pointed pencil had drawn them into the landscape. But the *sun*—that's the thing I couldn't take my eyes off of. It sat there in the sky, big and orange, just inches above the horizon. And that's what bothered me. It wasn't getting any closer to the ground. It hung where it was. No matter how long I watched, neither it nor the shadows ever moved.

My heart suddenly lurched. If it was nearly dusk, I'd been at the railroad tracks most of the day. I looked around. Where *were* Mike and Donny? If they'd gone for help, where was the ambulance? Why hadn't my parents come to get me? Surely they'd be worried by now. It didn't make any sense.

I'd better get home fast, I decided, and I went back to the bottom of the bank to follow the tracks toward Odyssey.

I hadn't gone far when I heard a *chugging* noise. It sounded like a steam engine approaching on the track behind me. But steam trains hadn't ridden on these tracks for years. Still, the sound was clear. And then came the whistle. I turned back to look. Just as I did, a black steam engine emerged from the blackness of the tunnel, white steam puffing up from its chimney.

"Far out," I said and stopped to watch it go past. I'd only seen a real steam engine in a museum. This one was shiny black all over except for the chrome connecting rods that pushed forward and backward on the wheels like arms and elbows. The engine was followed by the tender, which carried the fuel and water, followed by a couple of passenger carriages filled with—

I did a double take. The passenger cars were lit from inside, and I could make out clearly that they were filled with men in black-and-red uniforms. My first impression was that they looked like Nazis from an old war movie. But I knew that wasn't possible, either.

The passenger cars were followed by cattle cars. I began to count them, wondering who would be transporting cattle by an old steam engine, when I saw hands reaching out from between the wooden slats. My mouth fell open in shock. There were *people* in those cars, and not just a few. The carriages were jam-packed with them—hundreds, I figured. Many were crying out, shouting for help. I stumbled on a rock and fell to my knees, but my eyes never moved from those cattle cars.

More soldiers filled the caboose, and one who carried a rifle and stood outside, at the back railing, saluted me with a slight smile.

Are they prisoners? I wondered. *Is the train transferring inmates from one prison to another?*

I shook my head. Donny, Mike, and I had watched a lot of different kinds of trains go past Odyssey, but we'd never seen one carrying prisoners. At least, they'd never carried prisoners in a cattle car. I was sure that kind of thing was against the law. It was so cruel.

The train disappeared around the next bend, and for the first time I started to think I was in a dream. That made more sense than anything I'd seen so far. It certainly explained why the sun was still exactly where it had been 15 minutes ago. And why I'd seen that strange train. And why no one had come to look for me. Maybe I was at home asleep in my bed ... or maybe I was still knocked out in the tunnel, and even now Mike and Donny were trying to bring me around. Or maybe I was in the hospital.

I'd read stories about things like that—kids in comas having really vivid dreams. Maybe that's what was happening to me now.

I was getting more and more convinced of it the longer I walked. Nothing looked familiar. All the landmarks I'd expected to see were gone. There was no sign of Eddy's Convenience Store over near the highway, where Mike, Donny, and I had stopped to get sodas on our way to our spot by the tunnel. The highway wasn't there, either. And I couldn't find the field with the big oak tree that had a tire hanging from it on a rope. Or the intersection of Route 24 and Dixon's Road—probably because there was no Route 24 and no Dixon's Road to form an intersection.

I walked on and on, the sun hanging motionless in the sky, my mouth getting dry and my heart pumping harder and harder. I was growing scared now. Had I gone in the wrong direction? Even though I'd often gone down to the tracks to watch the trains, I had lived in Odyssey only a few months and might've lost my way.

Finally I found a dirt road that looked familiar and branched off from the tracks to follow it. I figured it would eventually take me to someone who might have a telephone. My feet kicked up the dirt in clouds of dust, which was weird. It had rained a lot the day before, yet this ground was bone-dry. And the grass on both sides of the road was as dead as if we'd been in a drought for years. In the distance, I could see forests of skeletal trees. I knew for a fact that the trees I'd seen earlier in the day were thick with green leaves. The road came to a small bridge that crossed what I assumed was a riverbed. It looked as if it hadn't seen water in ages.

At school I once saw a movie about the dust bowls of Oklahoma in the 1930s, where everything had turned brown, the water had dried up, and the people had been forced to move away or die. That's what this reminded me of. I half expected an old pickup truck to round the corner, driven by a man looking like Henry Fonda, except he wouldn't be a famous movie star but a poor, down-and-out guy with patches on his clothes and dirt smudged on his cheeks. And he'd have a thin wife with pinched eyes and a turned-down mouth, and she'd be carrying a hungry baby in her lap on the passenger side. There'd be five other kids with them, in rags, sitting in the back of the truck with a few pots and pans and a trunk of old clothes.

The road went on, seemingly forever. I was feeling panicked by now. I didn't see anything I recognized. No signs pointed me this way or that way. Everything was perfectly still in the setting sun that wouldn't set. I started to feel the sun was teasing me with a night that wouldn't come. I was getting hungry and thirsty, too.

Then I glanced at the barren field on my right and saw a bright-red, two-story farmhouse in the distance. My heart leaped with joy. Maybe someone there could help me. Maybe they would let me use the phone to call my parents to come and get me. I started to run toward the house, jogging at first and then picking up speed into a full run. As I got closer and closer, I noticed things that made my heart beat even faster. For example, the grass surrounding the house was thick and alive, spreading out like a green carpet. Clothes hung on a clothesline and gently moved in a breeze I couldn't feel. Fresh flowers grew in the flowerbeds around the porch and in boxes along some of the windows. Off to the side of the house stood a plot of vegetables. Everything had been so strangely empty and dead until now that the sight of normal life made me want to cry.

A woman came around the corner of the house carrying an empty basket. She was heavyset, her pale blouse and brown skirt billowing out from her like waterfalls. Her hair was tucked up under a scarf. She dropped the basket on the ground next to the vegetable garden and put her hands on her hips as if trying to decide what to pick for dinner.

"Hello!" I shouted.

The woman was startled and turned around quickly to face me. "What do you want?" she snapped as I came within a few feet. Her eyes were pinched and her mouth tugged down at the corners, and she looked as if she'd been through something terrible. She reminded me of one of the mothers I saw in that film about the Oklahoma dust bowls.

"I'm lost," I explained. "I'm trying to get back to Odyssey."

The woman shook her head. "I've never heard of it," she declared.

"It's a town somewhere around here."

The woman shook her head again. Then she did a curious thing. She took a step to one side as if she hoped to block my view of the garden behind her. I thought she looked nervous about it, as if I wasn't supposed to see it.

"Connellsville?" I asked. I was sure she must have heard of Connellsville. It was the biggest city in the area.

The woman shook her head again. "If this is some kind of prank, I won't put up with it," she warned.

"It's not," I said, my voice quivering without my meaning for it to. "I'm lost, and I need to call my parents. Can I use your phone?"

"Phone?"

"Yeah, your telephone. Please."

The woman looked at me as if I were speaking Swahili. Then her eyes widened as if she suddenly realized what I was saying. "Oh, one of those boxes that rings!" she exclaimed.

"Yeah!"

"I don't have one of those. Nobody around here does. Those are for the city people."

I felt like crying again. How was it possible that there was somebody left in the United States who didn't have a phone? Had I walked through some kind of time warp? I clenched and unclenched my fists, which is something I do to help me think. "If you've never heard of Odyssey or Connellsville, what city *is* around here?" I asked.

"Krawley is the closest city," she said, still keeping a watchful eye on me. "But that's miles away." Then she suddenly added: "There might be a ring box in Raundale."

"Raundale?" I'd never heard of it.

She nodded. "That's only a couple of miles from here."

A screen door slammed, and a young girl stepped out onto the porch. I figured she was about six years old. She had long, blonde hair and wore a flowered dress with a little apron. She had pale, white legs, white socks, and black shoes. I thought of Alice in Wonderland.

"Mama," she said.

The woman cut her off. "Go back inside, Cylindra," she ordered.

"But who is he?" the girl asked, pointing at me.

"I'm Scott," I answered, wanting to be friendly.

"Go back inside *right this minute*," the woman commanded.

The girl hesitated only a second, smiled at me, then turned and went back inside the house.

"You have to get to the main road," the woman said, turning her attention back to me and pointing in a different direction from the way I'd come. "Just follow my drive until it comes to the road. Turn right and you'll get to Raundale sooner or later."

"Thank you," I said, but I felt downhearted. The idea of walking several miles to a town I'd never heard of—one that might or might not have a "ring box"—was more than I could manage. I wanted to sit down for a minute. I wanted something to drink.

The woman must have realized how I felt because she said, "You look tired and worn out. Stay for a little while. Have a drink." She waved her hand nervously toward the garden. "You could join us for lunch."

"Thank you," I said again, relieved to be able to rest for a few minutes. "I'd love to have a drink, but I won't stay for—" I suddenly thought, *Lunch?* I looked at the sky. She must've meant to say "dinner."

The woman turned away and busied herself picking vegetables.

"May I help?" I asked, stepping around her to the edge of the garden.

"No, I'll do it," she said firmly. "No other hands but mine can touch this garden."

I stepped back. I knew people could be proud of their gardens, but not like this. "I won't hurt anything," I promised. "My mother grows vegetables, too, and I help her sometimes."

The woman snapped her head up. "Your mother grows vegetables?" she asked, seemingly amazed at the idea. "Where?"

"Behind our house," I answered, puzzled.

Her eyes narrowed as if she were trying to decide whether to believe me. "How does she grow vegetables?"

I shrugged. "Like everyone else does. In the ground. With seeds. And water."

The woman stood up, her hands back on her hips. "All right, who are you?" she demanded.

Her tone took me aback. What had I done wrong? "I'm Scott," I said.

"Did they send you here to spy on me? Is that it? Have they found out about me?"

"*They?* What *they?*" I asked, bewildered. "What are you talking about?"

Quick as lightning, she grabbed my ear and gave it a twist. "Then *how* does your mother grow vegetables?" she challenged.

"Ouch!" I cried out, turning my head in the direction of her twist until I thought I might fall over. "Cut it out!"

"Tell me!"

"She just *grows* them. I don't know how. You're hurting me!"

The woman probably would have twisted my ear off if we hadn't heard a car coming up the drive just then. "You've betrayed me," she whispered. She let go of my ear, and I suddenly found myself off balance. I fell onto my side in the dirt.

A large, black sedan with smoked windows approached.

CHAPTER TWO

———✦———

The woman moved quickly toward the house. I got the impression that she wanted to run inside, but the car arrived and pulled to a stop just as she reached the porch steps. It looked really official, like the kind that presidents and ambassadors ride in. This one looked a lot older, though, like the ones they used back in World War II. Several men got out. They wore the black-and-red uniforms I'd seen on the soldiers in the steam train.

The woman stopped where she was.

Another vehicle pulled up behind the car. It looked like a Jeep and had what looked like a machine gun mounted on the back. Another man in black and red sat behind the gun, his hand resting on it.

What in the world is going on here? I wondered. I got to my feet as fast as I could and tried to make sense of what I was seeing. It felt as if I'd walked in on somebody's movie, but nobody had told me what the movie was or what my part was supposed to be.

One of the men opened the rear passenger door of the limousine. With a great flourish, a short man with a shaved head and a thin, black mustache got out and walked toward the woman.

After looking her over, he asked formally, "You are Wydrah?"

"Who wants to know?" she replied defiantly.

"My name is Colonel Krake. I am here on the business of Supreme Commander Mobeck!" he barked. He waved a hand at his men and ordered, "I want samples of everything. The grass. Those flowers. The water in the well. And especially whatever she has growing in that garden." The men saluted and went off in separate directions. As an afterthought, the colonel shouted, "I believe I saw fruit trees on the other side of the house, too!"

One of the men, a soldier, came over to the garden and scowled at me. "Step aside," he ordered. I obeyed. He began pulling up carrots, potatoes, and sprouts and throwing them in Wydrah's basket.

"They'll do you no good," Wydrah stated.

"We'll see about that," Colonel Krake replied. "How long did you and Draven think you could get away with it? The rest of the world has suffered for over three years, and you have your own little paradise. Did you really think we wouldn't learn about your secret eventually?"

"I have done nothing wrong," Wydrah answered boldly. "Everything I have here is given by the hand of the Unseen One."

"Given by some technological trickery of *Draven*, you mean."

"He is the voice of the Unseen One. That he chose to bless me with—"

"Don't give me your religious mumbo jumbo," Krake growled. "You know it is against the law to even *think* such things, let alone speak them aloud."

"Make all the laws you want. You can't outlaw the truth."

Krake suddenly backhanded Wydrah across the face. The force of the blow knocked her aside, but she didn't fall. I was stunned for a moment, but then I instinctively started forward. I had been taught that a man should never hit a woman and that if one did, you stopped him from doing it again.

Firm hands gripped my shoulders. "Don't give it a second

thought," the soldier who had been pulling vegetables advised. I fumed but stayed where I was.

Wydrah stood her ground against Colonel Krake.

He smiled and pointed to the cut on her lip. A tiny sliver of blood formed and fell from it. "Will that go away in a matter of days or a matter of minutes?" he asked, apparently amused by what he'd done.

Wydrah didn't answer.

Krake clasped his hands behind his back and walked casually around the yard. "We'll see." He called out, "Draven!"

There was no reply. I stole a glance at the house and saw the corner of a curtain in one of the downstairs windows move. I caught a glimpse of the little girl who'd come out onto the porch earlier. Then she retreated.

"Draven!" Krake called again.

"He isn't here," said Wydrah.

"Where is he?"

"I don't know. He doesn't tell me his plans."

Krake studied her for a moment. "Why should I believe you?"

Wydrah held up her hands. "I have no reason to lie."

"To protect him. To protect your paradise."

"It isn't mine to protect. It belongs to the Unseen One."

Krake frowned at her. "According to our files, you weren't always so faithful to the false religion of the Unseen One. Your husband was Kendor, a valiant warrior in our nation's war with Monrovia."

"He was a valiant warrior—until Mobeck sent him to the salt mines of Dorman," she said scornfully. "He died there, leaving me with this farm and a daughter to take care of alone."

"Not alone," Krake said simply. "You've taken up with this traitor Draven."

"I haven't *taken up* with him," she corrected. "He came to me in need of lodgings, and that's what I gave him. He has a room in the basement."

Krake signaled another soldier. The soldier saluted, then marched up the steps and into the house. I assumed he was going to search Draven's room. Wydrah watched uneasily as the soldier went. I wondered if the little girl would hide.

"You won't find anything," Wydrah said. "He doesn't have any personal belongings."

"Leave that to us."

"Your men had better not break anything."

Krake ignored her challenge. "You mentioned your daughter. Where is she?"

"She went to the village to visit a friend."

"She left this paradise of food and water to go to the village? Why not invite the village to come here, to share in your good fortune?"

"There is only ever enough for three. No more, no less."

Krake hooked a thumb in my direction. "And what about this boy?"

"I assume he's one of your spies. He arrived only moments before you did."

Krake looked down his nose at me. "Don't be absurd. We don't send boys to do men's work. We tracked Draven to you by other means."

Wydrah seemed indifferent. "That boy means nothing to me either way. He's a stranger."

"I'm from Odyssey," I volunteered. "I was lost. I came here because I wanted to call my parents. Could you take me to a phone?"

Krake gazed at me as if I'd been hooting like an owl or gibbering like a chimpanzee. Then he turned back to Wydrah.

"So when did Draven come to you?"

"Over three years ago. Right after time stood still."

I was just about to feel offended that he'd ignored me when the phrase "right after time stood still" suddenly penetrated my brain. I wasn't sure I'd heard correctly. *Right after time stood still.* Yes, she had said it. I looked at Krake's expression to see if he'd reacted to it. He hadn't. He continued to talk as normally as if she'd said Draven had come right after a thunderstorm. I glanced over my shoulder at the soldier behind me. He hadn't reacted, either.

What does she mean? I wondered. I looked at the sky again. The sun was positioned exactly where it had been after I came out of the tunnel. How long ago was that? Two hours? Maybe three? And it hadn't moved. We had been on the edge of dusk all that time.

Right after time stood still.

I rubbed my temples. The bump on my forehead ached. My whole head hurt. And I still felt hungry and thirsty. None of this made sense.

"He was an enemy of the people and you gave him a place to live," Krake was saying when I started to pay attention again.

"I had no idea who he was then," Wydrah said defensively. "I am isolated on this farm."

"And he brainwashed you into believing in the Unseen One."

"When he arrived, I thought my daughter and I would die from starvation. Then, because of this man, my grass began to grow, my trees yielded fruit, and my vegetable garden came to life. How else could I explain it? It was as if time began again for us. My daughter has aged three years. I have lived normally. We thank the Unseen One for it all."

Krake paced around Wydrah and said derisively, "The rest of the world is trapped in frozen time, with a sun that doesn't rise or set, a day that doesn't change, pain that doesn't subside, and wounds that don't heal. No one is born, no one dies, everything is locked exactly where it was over three years ago when Draven somehow accomplished this witchcraft, and *you* are happy to—"

"Is everybody crazy?" I finally cried out.

All eyes turned to me.

"I can't take it anymore!" I shouted. "If this is somebody's idea of a bad joke, or this is the funny farm department of a nearby loony bin, or I've walked onto the set of a weird movie, then fine, you go ahead and play this game. But I want out of here! So somebody had better come up with a phone so I can call my parents *right now* or I'll have you all arrested for kidnapping!"

I was proud of my speech. It had the right tone and volume to be taken seriously.

"Jorgan," Krake said to the vegetable-picking soldier.

"Yes, sir," Jorgan replied.

I turned to see what he was going to do and got smacked across the face just as I did. I tumbled to the ground, feeling as if a swarm of bees had instantly taken over the inside of my head. With Wydrah's basket in hand, Jorgan stepped over me and walked back to Krake.

I closed my eyes and groaned. I suddenly wished this whole thing was a bad dream and I'd wake up in the tunnel again. No such luck. I slowly got to my feet.

The rest of the soldiers returned to Colonel Krake as well. They all had their samples, collected from around the farm. They looked confused and worried as they held out what they had found. "Colonel Krake," the first soldier said nervously.

"What is this?" Krake shouted angrily. He slapped at the man's hands.

"It was grass when I dug it up," the soldier explained fearfully, "but it immediately turned to this." He pointed to the handful of brown straw now lying in the dirt.

"What about the rest of you?" Krake frowned as he inspected what they'd brought. "These were apples, I suppose?"

A second soldier nodded. "They hung full and delicious on the trees, but they turned to this when I plucked them off." He looked a little green and added, "I tried to bite into one and got a mouthful of worms."

Krake grunted. The bucket from the well was filled with dust.

"I'm afraid it's true for everything, sir," the soldier who'd picked the vegetables said finally. He turned the basket upside down. Everything he'd put into it fell to the ground, rotten and dried out.

"Explain this," Krake demanded of Wydrah.

"I can't explain it," she replied. "All I know is that it can only be touched by my hand or it dies. It can't be taken away. It can't be used by anyone else."

Krake looked at her coolly. "I should arrest you now and tear this place apart." I waited, wondering if he would do it. Instead, he sighed and said, "But that won't help me find Draven, will it?"

"You won't find Draven unless he wants to be found."

Just then a commotion broke out at the front door. The soldier who'd gone in to search Draven's room had kicked open the screen door and stepped onto the porch. He was carrying a squirming Cylindra. She started to scream in protest. He roughly clasped his hand over her mouth.

"Leave her alone!" Wydrah shouted.

"In the village visiting friends?" Krake asked with a raised eyebrow. "What other lies have you told me?"

The soldier carrying Cylindra suddenly yelped as she bit his hand. He dropped her, and she scrambled to get away. He grabbed her by the nape of the neck and pulled her back again.

"Can't you keep control of a little girl?" Krake taunted the soldier.

The man, indignant at the jibe, jerked Cylindra to her feet and gave her a hard swat across the face. She tumbled down the steps, her head slamming against the corner of the bottom one. Then she lay still.

Wydrah was at her daughter's side in an instant. "Cylindra!" she cried out and cradled the limp child.

"We'll have to leave Draven a message," Krake said. He signaled his men back to the car, and they all got in. The engine roared to life, and the car sped away in a cloud of dust. The Jeeplike vehicle didn't move. The driver sat stone-faced. The soldier behind the mounted gun pulled the bolt back.

I felt fear like an electric jolt go through me, and I dropped to the ground.

The soldier opened fire, the machine gun roaring like a million jackhammers. But the gun wasn't aimed at any of us. It was pointed at the house, letting loose a terrible spray of bullets. They splintered the wooden posts on the porch, tore through the boards along the walls, and shattered the window glass.

Wydrah held Cylindra tight as she kicked and crawled to get away from the flying debris. On and on the explosion of gunfire went. It lasted only half a minute, probably, but it seemed like an hour. Finally it stopped. The sudden silence was like a roar in my ears. Then the Jeep's engine came to life, the gears were wrenched into place, and the vehicle sped away.

Wydrah sobbed and struggled to her feet. She clung to Cylindra as she stumbled toward the house. I leaped up and followed them onto the porch.

"Is she all right?" I asked.

The screen door hung by only one hinge now, and Wydrah kicked it aside to go in.

"I can get help," I offered. "I'll find an ambulance."

I stopped inside the front door, breathless at what I saw. The front room was devastated. Lamps were broken and tipped over. Framed paintings and photos hung cockeyed on the walls or had fallen off completely. In the corner, the banister to the stairs was fractured. The chairs and sofa had the stuffing bursting out of them.

"Tell me what to do!" I begged. But Wydrah didn't answer. Weeping, she carried her daughter straight over to what was left of the stairs. "Where can I go for help?" I pleaded again.

Without turning, she said softly, "You can't go for help." She then took the stairs carefully, one by one, up and out of my view.

The world spun away from me then. I felt weak and dizzy and put my hand up to balance myself on the arm of a chair. But I must have missed and felt myself clawing at thin air as I passed out.

CHAPTER THREE

The light of the never-ending dusk filled the room. I woke up with a dirty, metallic taste in my mouth. What I had hoped was a dream—the men in black and red, the sun frozen in the sky, the hurt girl—was all real. I was on the floor in the front room of Wydrah's bullet-ridden home. The house was silent except for a ticking clock. It sat on the mantle of a fireplace I hadn't noticed when I came in. Miraculously, the bullets hadn't hit the clock.

Its ticking was reassuring. It was normal. I stood up and went over to it. According to the dial, it was a little after two o'clock. Whether that meant two in the morning or two in the afternoon, I didn't know. I groaned and peered out one of the shattered windows. Yes, the sun stood exactly where it had been before. Morning or afternoon, it didn't seem to matter. And then I wondered how anyone could measure time in a place where time stood still? What was the use of clocks? Wasn't that like taking a boat to the desert?

I wondered if I should go upstairs to see if Cylindra had woken up. Or maybe Wydrah needed my help. She didn't want it before, though, so I decided I should leave them alone for now.

My eye caught sight of an old-fashioned radio sitting on a stand. It was wooden and domelike, with a long strip of station frequencies at the bottom. I tried the on-off knob. Nothing happened. Then I noticed that the bullets had destroyed the plug.

My mouth was dry. I needed a drink. I listened for any movement upstairs. When I didn't hear anything, I decided Wydrah wouldn't be upset if I helped myself to some water. I walked down a hall off the front room. It went past a couple of doors, then opened into a dining room. The bullet damage showed on the walls and table, but it wasn't as bad as in the front room.

I continued on to the kitchen. It looked nothing like any modern kitchen I'd ever seen. Instead, it reminded me of the kitchen in my grandparents' old house. It had a white basin sink with individual chrome knobs for hot and cold water. The refrigerator was also white and rounded and had a latch handle on the front. Rather than counters with cabinets, there were tables and a tall, wooden hutch with dishes inside. Amazingly, the bullets hadn't penetrated this far. It was as if the devastation hadn't occurred at all.

I found a glass and poured some water from the tap. As I drank it, I spied a stack of newspapers and magazines next to the back door. Curious, I picked them up and put them on the kitchen table to have a look. *Maybe they'll help me understand what's going on,* I thought.

The newspapers were yellowed copies of *The Sarum Times* and a smaller local paper called *The Raundale Gazette.* The magazines had glossy black-and-white photos on the front and featured names like *Our Life* and *Weekly News Digest.* They had white postage stickers on the bottom addressed to "Wydrah, Kendor's Farm-Near-Raundale."

The photo on the cover of one magazine showed a man dressed to the hilt in a military uniform and a woman dressed in a fancy gown, waving to a large crowd from a balcony. The man had slicked-back hair and a thin mustache. But it was the woman who caught my eye. She had the most beautiful face I'd ever seen. It was perfect. Her wide eyes seemed to stare at me directly. Her slender face was alive with a full smile that was just for me. The caption said it was "our Supreme Commander

Mobeck and his beautiful wife, Skalaw, the new First Lady of Sarum."

Eventually I tore myself away from that photo and flipped through the magazine. Then another. And another. And then a few more newspapers. Finally I felt certain that I wasn't in Odyssey anymore. I wasn't even in the same country. Worse, I wasn't in the same *world*.

One newspaper had a headline about Supreme Commander Mobeck taking control of the government, the military, and all utility companies. Another headline told of the eastern part of this country called Marus breaking off to establish its own government. Mobeck hadn't liked it, but he had lacked the military power at the time to stop it. The front page had a map of Marus. It was shaped like a large, lumpy potato, with a red line down the center to indicate how the nation had been divided. Even Sarum, the capital city, was divided in half. Border guards were placed on all major roads. It was as if Marus had had a civil war without any fighting.

The eastern part was governed as a democracy, with an elected president and congress. But the western part was ruled by Supreme Commander Mobeck and his wife. He was called "supreme commander" in the same way that Adolf Hitler had been called "chancellor" or "führer." It was just another name for *king*, I figured. They lived in a palace in the western part of Sarum.

I got the impression from the photos and articles that Mobeck and Skalaw were popular leaders. Everyone loved them and their ideas. They promised to bring the whole country into a new kind of civilization by getting rid of the old ideas, the old religions and superstitions, the old ways of thinking. They promised a new prosperity and true happiness for everybody.

In the name of progress, Mobeck had led his troops into the neighboring countries of Adria, Monrovia, and Gotthard. He had claimed it was his moral duty to unite all nations in enlightenment. To his annoyance, he hadn't been able to invade Palatia to the south or Albany to the north. They were allied with East Marus and would have proved too strong to fight at the time. But he was determined to build up his military power, and he might have succeeded by now, except for one problem. Well, one *person* who was a problem, I should say.

A man called Draven.

I saw a "rare" photo of him in one of the glossy magazines. He was a handsome man in an old-time movie-star way, like Errol Flynn or Clark Gable, with wavy hair and sharp eyes, a smiling mouth, and straight, white teeth. Strangely, according to the magazine, he had different-colored eyes. The magazine said, "Legend has it that the so-called voices of the Unseen One characteristically have different-colored eyes—one blue, the other green."

I studied the photo. He didn't look like the kind of man who could be a troublemaker. But, according to the government and the newspapers, he was. Apparently he kept badgering Mobeck and Skalaw about leading the nation away from belief in the Unseen One. He claimed that they worshiped the "false gods of progress, man, science, and technology." The Unseen One was the source of life and worthy of faith, Draven said, and everything else was beneath Him. (At this point, I figured that believing in the Unseen One must be the same as believing in God. They sure sounded the same.)

Mobeck had tried to have Draven arrested, but no one could catch him. He seemed to escape easily to East Marus. This had made Mobeck want to attack that country all the more, but time had worked against him. Literally.

"Draven to Stop Time," announced the headline. The article then said that Draven had announced how the Unseen One was going to show His strength to the world by stopping time. "Then you will know and believe," Draven had said.

What happened next filled the newspapers and magazines. In the seventh hour after noon on the seventh day in the seventh month, the sun had stopped where it was in the sky. And everything had stopped with it. Nature had stopped. The seasons had stopped. The weather no longer changed. People stayed in whatever condition they were in at that moment. Hair and fingernails stopped growing. Everyone stopped aging. If people were sick, they stayed sick. If people were well, they couldn't get sick. Even if you tried to kill someone, let's say by stabbing or shooting, he or she would feel the pain, but the wounds would heal almost instantly.

I rubbed my eyes and tried to imagine what it had been like. Everyone and everything was exactly the same as at the moment time stopped. Yet people still went through the routines of eating, sleeping, waking up, and working.

The consequences were terrible. The sick suffered without dying. For a while, since the threat of being hurt didn't seem to bother hardened criminals, riots broke out and crime was rampant. The police didn't know how to stop people from breaking the law. Eventually the government set up a system of prisons and labor camps. Mobeck reasoned that bullets might not kill, but bodies could still be locked in chains and cells. He also figured out that pain was still pain, even though the healing might come quickly, so he made torture a feature of lawful punishment.

Because nature stood still, all the fields and trees gave up whatever they'd been growing at that moment. Crops that were ready to harvest were picked. But all those that weren't ready remained unusable, inedible. Crops couldn't grow. Fruit couldn't ripen. So the food supply had steadily dwindled. The government had taken over the fields and orchards to distribute the available food to everyone, but it had begun to run out after the second year.

Water supplies had also started to dwindle because it wasn't raining when time stopped, so there was no rain to replenish them. (I guess if it had been raining at that moment, it would be raining even now and everything would be soaked and flooded.)

My head started to hurt from thinking it through. Did all this mean clothes couldn't change? If they were rags then, were they rags now? If they were new then, were they new now? Could a car be crashed, or did the dents fix themselves right away? Did tools wear out? Could trees be cut down? How far did this whole time stoppage go?

I stared at the newspapers and magazines and tried to take it all in.

A few things made sense to me now. The steam train I'd seen when I first came out of the tunnel must have been taking people to prison or work camps. When Colonel Krake hit Wydrah in the mouth, he'd said something about whether she would heal quickly. She hadn't.

So somehow, for some reason, this little farm stood outside time. Wydrah had said it was a miracle brought about because of Draven. Vegetables grew, and fruit ripened. She and her daughter had even aged in the past three years.

I thought about the miracle and how it now worked against Wydrah. Bullets had destroyed part of the house, and it didn't repair itself. The soldier hurt Wydrah's daughter, and she was not healed.

My thoughts were suddenly interrupted by a sound from

upstairs. Someone was walking. I got up and followed the sound of footsteps across the upstairs floor, over to the stairs, then down to the front room. There I met up with Wydrah. She looked dazed. Her eyes were red as if she'd been crying the whole time she was up there.

I opened my mouth to ask about Cylindra, but Wydrah spoke first. "I will pick some vegetables for our supper," she said. Her tone was flat and the words mechanical. She then walked quietly toward the front door.

"But what about Cylindra?" I asked. "How is she?"

Wydrah paused at the door, her back to me. "My daughter is dead," she said, and then she left.

CHAPTER FOUR

In spite of my protests, Wydrah insisted on fixing us a meal. "It will go to waste otherwise," she said firmly, and she went about preparing the food. We ate at the kitchen table in silence. Afterward, she brushed the shards of glass and chips of wood off the sofa in the front room and made it as comfortable as she could for me. "You'll sleep here until we can figure out what to do with you," she explained. Then she spread sheets and blankets across the torn cushions.

"I'm sorry about Cylindra," I tried to say when I lay down, but the words caught in my throat and were choked out as a squeak. I swallowed hard and continued. "I'm not a spy. I don't even belong here."

"I know," she replied. She went back upstairs.

It was past nine according to the clock on the mantle. I was exhausted, but my mind spun with what I'd seen in the newspapers and magazines. Then the day's events wove their way into my thoughts and I remembered the tunnel; the steam train; the long, endless walk that led me to the farm; the Nazi-like soldiers; and the machine gun. I thought of Cylindra lying somewhere upstairs. I imagined Wydrah weeping over her daughter. The scenes and images replayed again and again in my head and burned like a fever.

A sound like a closing door made me jump. I didn't think I'd fallen asleep, but I had. The clock said it was now a little before one o'clock. I sat up on the sofa and listened. Someone was in the kitchen ... coming through the dining room ... and now walking lightly down the hall. I got to my feet just as he stepped into the front room.

"Well!" a man said. "What happened here?" He moved into the room and surveyed the damage.

Though he seemed a little older than he had in the photos, there was no mistaking who it was—Draven. His wavy hair was graying at the temples, and the lines around his eyes were etched more deeply. He was tall—well over six feet, I thought. He wore a tweed jacket with a white shirt and vest underneath and brown trousers. His clothes were rumpled and looked as if he'd been wearing them a long time. The outfit reminded me of the kinds of suits my father wore to his job as a philosophy professor at Campbell College—all except for his shoes: Draven had on black, knee-high boots.

He fixed his gaze on me. Even in that dusk light, I could see that his eyes were different colors. One was green, and the other was blue. It was startling at first, but then I remembered what the magazine had said about it.

"I was wondering when you would show up," he said to me, as if he'd been waiting for my arrival.

I was going to ask what he meant, but just then Wydrah came down the stairs. She was in a robe now, her hair disheveled. Somehow she looked a lot older than she had before.

Draven took one look at her and a shadow crossed his face.

Wydrah crossed the room in an instant and was on him, weeping and pummeling him with her fists. "It's all your fault!" she screamed. "My daughter is dead and it's all your fault!"

Draven struggled to catch her arms. "Stop, Wydrah," he said gently.

"Why didn't you kill us right away?" she cried. "It would have been better than this! They came looking for you!"

Draven got hold of her arms and pulled her close. She collapsed against him, sobbing into his chest. He caressed her hair and patted her back, whispering comfort in her ear. Then I realized that he had also begun to cry. "I'm sorry," he said over and over.

Wydrah calmed down and stood away from him. Her voice took on its normal strength. "I took you in. I gave you a home. I never asked questions. I believed you when you said the Unseen One would protect us. But now ..."

"I know," Draven said, his deep voice thick with his own tears. "I didn't know this would happen."

"You didn't know?" Wydrah was aghast.

"No, I didn't," he replied, shaking his head. "How could I? I am not the Unseen One who sees all and knows all. I'm only His voice."

Wydrah glared at him for a moment, then said sternly, "I want you to leave this house. Now."

Draven looked as if she'd slapped him across the face. After a moment, he recovered his composure enough to warn, "You'll die."

"So what? I don't want to live without my daughter."

He glanced away as if something outside had caught his eye. Then he said, "I'll go. But I must see her first."

Wydrah looked as if she might refuse him. But she must have thought better of it because she nodded and told him, "She is lying in her room."

Draven went past us and up the stairs. Wydrah didn't move but stood with her arms folded across her chest. I sat back down on the sofa and waited. I imagined Draven was going to pay his last respects. He felt bad, I could tell. The only reason the soldiers came to the house was to find him, so it was his fault in a way. But then I felt sorry for him because he couldn't have known the soldier would slap Cylindra. No one could have anticipated that she'd fall and hit her head like that.

I watched Wydrah, who didn't budge. I thought about saying something to defend Draven, to remind her that he wasn't entirely to blame. But I didn't know what to say. In a sense, it wasn't my place to say anything. I was the stranger. I didn't belong here. And it came to my mind that I should probably leave, too.

But where was I supposed to go? Back to the tunnel with the hope of finding my way home?

We waited. After a while, I thought I heard the sound of a man crying. My heart sank.

Wydrah stiffened as we heard Draven returning. He came down the stairs, carrying Cylindra in his arms. She was still. I stood up, unsure what was going to happen next.

"How dare you!" Wydrah cried. "You have no right to touch my child!"

Suddenly the girl lifted her head. "Mommy!" she exclaimed, smiling and stretching out her arms.

Wydrah gasped, her face a mixture of shock and amazement. "Cylindra?"

"Were you crying?" her daughter asked.

Collecting Cylindra in a scoop of her arms and with a close hug, Wydrah answered, "Yes, yes, but it's all right now." She began to cry again anyway.

Draven stood at my side, and we watched Wydrah dance her daughter around the room in joy.

"That nasty man knocked me down and I hit my head," Cylindra said, "but I feel better now."

"How is this possible?" Wydrah asked as she stopped her dance and sat Cylindra on the couch. She inspected the girl's head, placed a hand to her heart, checked her pulse, and then touched her lightly all over as if she couldn't believe her daughter was truly alive. Then she looked up at Draven. "I didn't make a mistake. She was dead."

"Thank the Unseen One," said Draven.

Wydrah threw herself at his feet. "Forgive me," she begged. "I'm sorry for what I thought, for what I said."

Draven knelt down, lifted her chin with a finger, and smiled at her, but he didn't speak.

"Never in the history of the world has this happened," Wydrah said. "Has anyone ever come back from the dead?"

I was aware that Cylindra was looking at me. "What is she talking about?" she asked in a small voice.

"You'd better ask her later," I answered with a shrug. I was tempted to reach out to touch her head, to feel her temperature. To be honest, I think I wanted to make sure she wasn't some kind of ghost. But she smiled at me—the same way she'd smiled earlier—and I knew she was the same girl. Whatever had happened, she seemed in perfect health.

Draven, meanwhile, lifted Wydrah to her feet. "We have to leave," he told her.

She looked crestfallen. "I didn't mean what I said before," she said pleadingly. "You can stay as long as you want."

"Thank you," he replied, "but I really do have to leave. Come on."

To my surprise, Draven's "come on" was addressed to me. "Me? You want me to come with you?" I asked.

"Why else do you think you're here?"

"But what about us?" Wydrah asked. "If you go now, we'll be doomed."

Draven put a reassuring hand on her shoulder as he said, "You'll be all right."

"But—"

"Trust in the Unseen One." Draven waved a hand at me and stepped out onto the front porch. "Go to bed, both of you," he said to them over his shoulder. "You must be very tired."

I started to follow him, then turned quickly to Wydrah and Cylindra. I didn't know what to say to either of them. "Thanks for everything," I finally managed with a burning blush. "It was nice meeting you."

But, strangely, Wydrah was sitting on the sofa with Cylindra, and they both looked as if they were about to slump over, asleep.

I rushed after Draven, who was now walking toward the field. "What's going to happen to them?" I asked when I caught up with him.

"They'll sleep and awaken with only the memory of a bad dream."

"But the house ..."

"What about it?"

"You saw it," I answered. "It's a wreck."

"Is it?"

I was confused. "Isn't it?"

"You tell me."

I looked back at the house to confirm the damage I knew was there, and then I stopped dead in my tracks. The splintered wood, the shattered windows, the screen door that had hung by a single hinge—everything was fixed, just like it was when I had first arrived.

I gaped at Draven. "Are you a magician?" I asked.

Draven frowned back at me. "Don't ever refer to the Unseen One's doings as magic. It's an insult." Then he turned and walked on.

"I'm sorry," I said, picking up my pace to stay with him.

"But I'm really confused about what's going on here."

"What are you confused about?"

I was at a loss for where to begin. "Well … *everything*."

"You're going to have to be more specific."

"Back at Wydrah's house, you acted like you knew me."

"I don't *know* you. In fact, I don't even know your name. But I knew you were the one who was supposed to help me. So what's your name?"

"I'm Scott," I answered. "But how am I supposed to help you? I don't belong here."

"Of course you belong here. The Unseen One wouldn't have brought you if you didn't belong here."

"Then you've got me confused with someone else. I'm not from this world," I explained, the words sounding unbelievable even as I said them. "I'm from Odyssey. I went into a tunnel and—"

Draven waved a hand at me. "You're talking about incidentals. This world, that world, what does it matter? Marus has a long history of receiving help from unusual places. It was a boy like yourself who brought the judgment of the Unseen One to Marus in the days of Arin. A mysterious child from another world traveled with our patriarch Marus himself when he came to this country on the instructions of the Unseen One. Another boy from another world helped Glennall save this world from great famine. Three children from another world brought the signs that helped Fendar in the days when our people were slaves to the Palatians. And there are many more examples. You are what we now call *giftbearers*."

"Giftbearers?"

"Yes. You come bearing gifts that help the people of faith fulfill the purposes of the Unseen One."

"Are you saying that *I'm* a giftbearer?"

"You may prove to be more than that," Draven said cryptically.

"But I don't belong here," I insisted. "I have a mother and a father in my world."

"And I had a mother and father once, too. But often our callings take us away from them. It's the sacrifice we must make."

"Nobody asked me if I wanted to make that kind of sacrifice."

Draven stopped short there in the middle of the field and turned to face me. "I'll ask you now. Do you want to continue with me or go back to your world? Say the word and you'll be returned."

I was surprised by the offer. Did I want to go back now? I had to think about it a moment. "I want to go back, but ..." I hesitated.

"But?"

"But first, can you tell me what I'll miss if I leave?"

"The mighty works of the Unseen One. A time of miracles. Or you may miss nothing at all. How can I answer that question? None of us get any guarantees from the Unseen One about the future."

I frowned as I clenched and unclenched my fists. "Do I have to decide right this minute? Can't I go along with you for a little while longer?"

"I can't promise your safe return if you stay. From this point on, everything will move dangerously fast. We are going to Sarum to confront Mobeck. Anything can happen to us."

"You mean ... he might kill us?"

"He'd like to kill *me*, I know that for sure." Draven looked off to the horizon. "I have a train to catch. Are you coming with me or not?"

He didn't wait for my answer but strode onward.

I was frozen by indecision. I could go home right now and carry on as I always had. Or I could stay here and play out what I knew would be an adventure. The choice felt agonizing. It seemed the same as asking Wendy not to go with Peter Pan. Or asking Peter, Lucy, Edmund, and Susan not to go to Narnia. Or asking that Connecticut Yankee guy not to go to King Arthur's court.

Draven disappeared over the next ridge.

"Wait!" I shouted and raced after him.

CHAPTER FIVE

We reached the railroad tracks just as a freight train chugged alongside. "This one will do," Draven said as he broke into a jog. I ran behind him, being careful to stay clear of the wheels and tracks. He reached out to an open door, grabbed the handle, and pulled himself up. He then held his hand out to me. "Take hold!" he shouted.

I was feeling winded, and for a fraction of a second, I wasn't sure I'd make it. But then his hand, strong and sure, caught mine and hoisted me aboard.

The car was empty and dirty. Draven went to the far end and dropped onto a small cushion of hay. With his hands tucked behind his head, he looked the picture of comfort. I dropped down next to him.

"What now?" I asked.

"Sleep," he said. "I'll wake you when it's time."

I lay back into the hay and let the gentle bounce of the car and the sound of the wind going past the door lull me to sleep. It must've been a deep sleep. I don't remember dreaming or sensing any change around me until, somewhere in my slumbers, I was aware that all had gone still. I opened my eyes. Draven stood at the door, his hands shoved deep in his coat pockets. I stretched, and he turned to me.

"Good morning," he said with a smile. "I was just about to wake you."

"We stopped."

Draven nodded. "So we have. Which means it's time to get

off and find better accommodations." With that, he leaped down from the car.

I got up and sluggishly followed, brushing at the hay on my clothes and in my hair as I went. From the door, I could see that we'd reached a major station. Lines of railway cars sat on more tracks than I could count.

"This way," Draven called out from my left.

I scrambled down and skipped back and forth among the long, iron rails and thick, wooden ties to keep up with him. Together we ducked around another freight train and took some stairs that led down into an underpass. It seemed to stretch for a mile, with stairs leading up from it to various station platforms. Draven finally saw the number he wanted and gestured for me to follow him up the corresponding flight of stairs. At the top, we came to the door of a car in a long passenger train. Draven opened it and gestured for me to board.

"But we don't have any tickets, do we?" I asked.

He gave me a gentle nudge. "It's been taken care of," he said.

I got on board and looked around. We were in a small passageway. I whispered, "Yeah, but aren't you a wanted man? Won't people be looking for you?"

Draven chuckled and pointed me toward the front of the train. "I can be found easily enough, if you know where to look," he answered.

We walked through the cars. Other passengers were getting on, putting their luggage in the overhead or underseat compartments. "Aren't we going to sit down?" I asked.

"Sure," he replied. "In the dining car."

"A dining car?" I wondered aloud. "What kind of dining car can you have in a terrible famine?"

"An expensive one."

And it was—a car in the middle of the first-class section with white tablecloths and silver salt and pepper shakers. We slid into a small booth.

A porter dressed in a sharp, red uniform and cap suddenly appeared and eyed us warily. "We won't be serving until 15 minutes after the train departs," he informed us.

Draven nodded and replied, "Thanks. We're meeting the minister of religious affairs."

The porter scrutinized us further. I picked a piece of hay from my hair. "If you say so," he finally sniffed and walked away.

"The minister of what?" I asked Draven. I felt as though I was spending all my time asking questions lately.

"You'll see."

We then sat in silence. I fiddled with the salt and pepper shakers. Draven kept his hands folded serenely on the table, his gaze fixed on the trains outside. I watched the people moving to and fro on the platform. Many looked down-and-out, with ragged clothes and gaunt faces. I also kept an eye on those who walked past us in the car. I expected someone in a black-and-red uniform to recognize Draven at any moment and rush in to arrest him. But no one did. No one paid him or me any attention at all.

Eventually the conductor blew a whistle on the platform and gave the signal for the train to leave. It lurched forward, then moved slowly away from the platform. Soon we were well on our way to wherever we were now going. I didn't know. And, tired of pestering Draven with so many questions, I decided not to ask.

Suddenly he said, "Ah."

I looked up. A bald, heavyset man in a dark, three-piece suit sauntered into the car. He was so busy trying to navigate himself around a food cart that he didn't see us. But then he lifted his eyes and caught sight of Draven. The effect was immediate. His eyes went wide, his face went white, and his jowls quivered. He glanced nervously at the porter, who was wiping glasses, and then around the empty car and tried to approach us casually.

"Sit down, Ladan," Draven said with a large smile.

"Are you crazy?" Ladan asked, his jowls still quivering. "Are you trying to get arrested?"

Draven ignored him. "Scott, I'd like you to meet Ladan. He's Supreme Commander Mobeck's right-hand man when it comes to religion in our lovely country. His *token* priest."

"Hi," I said.

"Nice to meet you," Ladan said quickly and then scooted in next to me on the bench. "Draven—"

"Are you going to order?" the porter asked, suddenly appearing again.

"No!" Ladan snapped.

"I'd like to order," Draven announced. "And I'm sure Scott is hungry, too."

I admitted I was starving.

"What do you have?" Draven asked the porter.

The porter sighed impatiently and produced three menus. I looked one over and saw that it had breakfasts of powdered eggs, fabricated meats, and artificial juices. So that was how they tried to cope with the crisis: The scientists came up with alternative foods. "Is the food any good?" I asked.

"As good as you'll get anywhere," Draven replied.

I shrugged and asked for their "hearty breakfast platter" of something resembling pancakes. Draven asked for eggs, bacon, and coffee. Ladan didn't want anything and waved the porter away impatiently.

Once the porter had gone, Ladan leaned on the table to face Draven. "What are you up to?" he demanded in a harsh whisper.

"What are *you* up to?" Draven countered. "Why aren't you at the palace, kowtowing to Mobeck?"

Ladan looked embarrassed and answered, "I'm on a mission for him."

"A mission!" Draven said, obviously pretending to be impressed. "To do what?"

Ladan lowered his head. "To find food for his horses."

Draven threw his head back and laughed loudly.

Ladan ignored him. "I've been scouring the north part of the country while Mobeck scours the south."

"You've been in the north for the past few days? What a coincidence. Some of Mobeck's goons came looking for me there and nearly killed a little girl in the process."

"It had nothing to do with me."

"Didn't it?"

"No. How could it? I never know where you are from one minute to the next. I don't *want* to know. I wish I didn't know now."

Just then, two officers dressed in black and red entered the car. Ladan gasped. "May the Unseen One have mercy!" he whispered.

The two men nodded to the porter and even saluted Ladan, but they didn't acknowledge Draven and me at all. I began to think we were invisible. They sat down at a table at the far end of the car and chatted amiably.

Ladan rubbed his face with a napkin. "This is more than my heart can take," he said miserably.

"You should lay off the fabricated cholesterol," Draven joked.

"What do you want from me, Draven?"

"I want you to deliver a message to Mobeck."

"Oh, no."

"Tell him I want to meet him."

"*What?*" Ladan reacted so loudly that the two officers turned to look at him. He cleared his throat and smiled at them. The porter returned with our breakfasts and set them on the table. I sniffed the so-called pancakes and frowned. They looked and smelled like nothing I'd ever seen before. I carefully poked at them with a fork and then tried them in small portions. They tasted like a pair of old socks.

Draven, meanwhile, ate his food as if it was the best he'd had in a long time.

Ladan drank some artificial water. "You want to *meet* Mobeck face-to-face?" he asked incredulously.

Draven nodded. "That's right. Ten o'clock tomorrow morning on the Field of the Great Kings. I assume you remember where that is."

"The royal park between Sarum and Hailsham," Ladan replied.

"At Maiden's Bridge."

Ladan shook his head. "Mobeck will throw me in the work camps if I deliver a message from you."

"No, he won't."

"What if you don't show up?"

"I'll be there."

"You say that, but you don't always know. What if the Unseen One whisks you away like He's done in the past? Mobeck will execute me." Ladan groaned.

"I'll be there."

"Why should I believe you?"

"What if I gave you a guarantee?"

Ladan raised an eyebrow. "What kind of guarantee?"

"I'll send my protégé with you."

"Him?" Ladan asked, gesturing to me.

I nearly gagged on the pancakes. "But what if he sends *me* to a work camp?" I sputtered.

Draven leaned back and leveled a steady gaze at us. "The two of you are going to have to trust me. Just as I trust the Unseen One."

"What if Mobeck won't agree to meet with you?"

"He will."

"Why?"

"Because this is the final showdown," Draven said as he dropped his napkin onto his plate. "The Unseen One is going to restore time."

Ladan gaped at Draven.

Draven scooted out of the booth and stood up. "Tomorrow morning at Maiden's Bridge."

I made a move, hoping to get Ladan to let me out.

"Stay where you are," Draven said. "Finish your meal. Enjoy the first-class compartment."

"But—"

"I'll see you tomorrow morning."

The officers at the other table now seemed to be taking notice of Draven. They looked at him carefully, then leaned their heads together in close whispers. Draven nodded to me and Ladan and then walked out of the car through the opposite door.

"Where's he going?" I asked. "Will he jump off the train or hide away somewhere?"

"More than likely he'll simply disappear," Ladan said with a sigh. "It's what he always does."

CHAPTER SIX

The train took us past rolling fields and villages, and then the houses and buildings came closer and closer together until we arrived at the city of Sarum, the capital of Marus. A long, black limousine, looking like something from our 1940s and much like Colonel Krake's car—a thought that made me shudder—met us at the front of the large terminal and drove us to the palace.

The city itself went by in a blur of wide avenues lined with barren trees, large buildings with tall pillars, massive statues of posturing heroes, cathedral-like department stores, and closed restaurants. Many of the buildings had large, black-and-red flags hanging from them. Each had a strange design of a snake curling up a green-leafed tree.

Ladan had been broody and quiet the entire trip, and I was hesitant to ask any questions. But my curiosity got the better of me. "What does that mean?" I asked him, pointing to the insignia.

Ladan looked at me with surprise. "What are they teaching you kids in school?" he asked rhetorically. "That's the national emblem of West Marus."

"But what does it mean?"

Ladan sighed impatiently. "A story has been told about the original man and woman and how the Unseen One had given them the rule of the world's original paradise."

"Adam and Eve?" I asked.

"I don't believe they were ever named," Ladan corrected me. "But a serpent in the tree persuaded them that knowledge and glory in an unknown world were greater than being servants in the Unseen One's paradise, and so they revolted and lost paradise."

"So why did Mobeck put that on a flag?"

"Because Mobeck agrees with the serpent. He believes in the ideal of Marutian Enlightenment—that Marutians are genetically superior to all other races. He believes we are destined to rule the world through science, technology, and faith in the future of Marus."

I looked at the people as they crowded the sidewalks and streets, many with the same rags and gaunt faces I'd seen before, and wondered if they would agree.

Ladan was also looking out the window and said hopefully, "But I believe that deep in his heart, Mobeck believes in and fears the Unseen One." Then, as if to answer the question I hadn't asked, he added, "But he also fears his wife and loves power too much to acknowledge his faith."

We turned through some large gates and followed the driveway up to the palace. The main building had a golden rotunda with something on top that might have been an angel. The palace then stretched to the left and the right, pointing to a great lawn on one side and forest on the other.

More men in black and red opened the car doors and led us into the palace itself. We went through an arched doorway into a foyer filled with paintings, statues, and a marble staircase that curved up to the next floor. A banner of the serpent in the tree hung like a giant curtain over everything. We then turned down a lush, paneled hallway filled with more paintings, artwork, and flags.

"Where is he?" Ladan asked one of the soldiers.

"The great hall," came the soldier's reply. "He and Lady Skalaw are preparing for the banquet tonight."

"What banquet?" Ladan inquired.

"He is having a state banquet for all his advisers," the soldier said, looking surprised. "Weren't you told?"

Ladan sighed again, the weight of the world on his shoulders. "Of course I wasn't told. I was too busy looking for horse feed in the north."

The great hall was great, indeed, with high walls and tall, triangular windows. The ceiling was covered with painted scenes of battles involving men on horseback, cannons, ships, tanks, and airplanes.

The beautiful woman I'd seen on the magazine cover stood in the middle of a sea of tables, all being laid for a grand banquet. Watching her for a moment, I thought she was more beautiful than the picture could have shown. She looked majestic, standing there in a long, golden gown.

"Not there!" she hissed at a servant. "Put it on the other side."

"Yes, Lady Skalaw," the servant said and moved a vase of artificial flowers to another part of the table.

The man I saw on the magazine cover, Supreme Commander Mobeck, sat in a chair on the stage at the far end of the hall. He watched his wife and the servants with undisguised boredom, but he brightened when Ladan approached.

"Ladan!" he exclaimed, leaping to his feet and moving to the edge of the stage. "Good news for my horses, I hope. They're going to die from that fabricated hay if we don't do something."

Ladan saluted. "I'm afraid my mission was fruitless," he reported. "The north country is barren."

"Confound it!" the supreme commander shouted and kicked at a microphone stand. It tipped and fell with a crash. "There was nothing in the south, either."

"Is something wrong, dear?" Lady Skalaw asked as she approached.

Mobeck growled and turned away from her like a child.

"No hay for his horses?" Skalaw asked Ladan.

Ladan shook his head.

Skalaw looked at me with cold, gray eyes. "Who is this vagrant?" she demanded.

Ladan swallowed nervously. "He is here as part of a message."

"Oh?" Mobeck asked and came around to face us again. "A message from whom?"

"From Draven."

"Draven!" Skalaw shrieked.

"By the two moons!" Mobeck exclaimed.

"It would be better if I explained in private," Ladan advised. His jowls were shaking again, and his skin had gone pasty.

"This way." Mobeck climbed down from the stage and signaled for his wife and Ladan to follow him. They retreated to a corner of the hall, where they huddled together. I waited where I was, catching my reflection in one of the shiny silver plates that dotted the length of both sides of a long table. I looked tired and dirty.

Ladan, Mobeck, and Skalaw whispered loudly. I couldn't make out any of the words, but the hisses rose and fell as if someone were slowly letting the air out of the building.

"By the two moons!" Mobeck shouted again at one point.

At another point, Skalaw clenched her fists and yelled, "He'll get more than he bargained for!"

After a few minutes, Mobeck and Skalaw slipped out through a door that was nearly hidden in a wall panel. Ladan came back to me. "That went better than I expected," he said, relieved.

"They aren't going to send us to a work camp?" I asked.

"Or kill us," he replied, dabbing at his sweaty forehead with a handkerchief. "They've gone off to talk to other advisers. Meanwhile, let's find you a room and a bath."

We walked down one corridor after another until we came to Ladan's private apartment, which consisted of a series of interconnected rooms. I noticed one with a bed, another with a big desk and bookcases jammed with books, and another that looked like a living room. I don't know how many rooms there were, but Ladan took me down a hallway to one, about the size of a closet, with a single bed.

"I'll have my servant help you with a bath," he said. He sniffed the air and added disdainfully, "And we'll find you some fresh clothes."

I sat on the edge of the bed to take off my sneakers. A minute later, a tall, thin man with smiling eyes and a mop of white hair came in. "My name is Adimah, and I'm here to make you presentable," he announced. He dropped a robe onto the bed. "Change into that while I have your clothes cleaned."

"Where is Ladan?" I asked.

"He has things to do," Adimah explained. "If you need anything or have any questions, simply ask me." Then he left the room.

I got out of my dirty clothes and put on the robe. It was thick and soft.

"I'm drawing you a bath," Adimah said when he returned to get my clothes a minute later. "It's reconstituted water, so I wouldn't swallow it or get it in my eyes if I were you."

"I'll be careful."

Adimah led me down the hall to a bathroom. In the center was a long, white, claw-footed tub filled to the top with bubbles.

"Pull that cord by the door if you need me," he said as he closed the door behind me. I got into the bathtub and slid into the hot water and bubbles. It was like burrowing into a sleeping bag that had been sitting next to a roaring fire all night. It was perfect. I leaned back and closed my eyes.

A few minutes later, I heard the latch click and a gentle squeak of the hinges as the door opened. I glanced over, expecting to see Adimah again. Instead, a man with thick, black hair and a scowling face came at me with his hands held out. I shouted, but the big hands were on me, pushing me down into the water. Once, then twice, and then a third time. I gasped for air as I was dragged out of the tub and thrown onto the floor.

"Get dressed," the man said in a low, thick voice.

I grabbed the robe just in time for him to give me a hard push toward the door. He jabbed and shoved me into the living room, went to the far corner, and gave a panel in the wall a nudge. It opened. Yanking at my robe, he dragged me into a dark passageway and then down a labyrinth of secret corridors. We finally reached another hidden doorway, which he somehow opened before pushing me into a dimly lit room that had a small, wooden desk and two chairs.

"Sit down," he said and left the room.

Soaked and shivering, I sat on one of the chairs. I considered trying to run back into the secret passageway, but I knew I would get hopelessly lost, so I waited.

Ten, maybe 15 minutes went by, and then a regular door opened on the other end of the room. Lady Skalaw entered with a poise and flourish that reminded me of an actress on a stage. She crossed to the desk and sat down in the chair opposite to me. Again I was struck by how beautiful she was. Her face was pale and slender, her mouth full and round. Her eyes, dark gray, seemed as if they looked through me. Her brown hair hung around her face like a halo of dark light.

"So you are Scott," she began with a smile. "I am Lady Skalaw."

"I know," I stammered, swallowing hard. "I saw your picture in a magazine. Not one picture, I mean. I saw a lot of pictures in the magazines. Then I saw you in the great hall." I blushed and felt like an idiot.

"You're shivering," she observed. "I'll turn up the heat while your clothes are brought." She waved a finger as if to alert someone.

That's when I noticed the large mirror on the wall. It was one of those two-way mirrors, I figured. Then I wondered how many people were watching us—and why. "Have I done something wrong?" I asked.

"I don't know," she responded. "Have you?"

"That man dragged me out of my bathtub and brought me here."

"Don't mind Tesdor. He's clumsy and has no sense of timing. But I asked him to bring you to me so we could talk. You want to talk to me, don't you?"

I gazed at her face. "If you want me to."

"Tell me about Draven."

"What about him?"

"Where is he now?"

"I don't know. He didn't tell me where he was going."

"Then why were you traveling with him?"

"Because he asked me to."

Lady Skalaw paused for a moment, as if reconsidering her questions. "Let's start at the beginning. How and when did you meet him?"

"I met him yesterday." I hesitated, suddenly unsure of

myself. "At least, I think it was yesterday. I was lost and came to a farmhouse where some soldiers showed up and hurt a little girl who died, and then they shot up the house with bullets."

"A little girl died?" Skalaw asked with a stern look at the mirror.

"Yes, ma'am. But Draven came and brought her back to life."

Lady Skalaw was silent, but I could feel her eyes on me. Her lips were still fixed into a charming smile. "Draven brought a dead girl back to life?"

"Yes, ma'am."

She chuckled. "You're mistaken, I'm sure."

"No. He did."

"You're certain about that. You saw for yourself that the girl was dead. A doctor came and pronounced her dead. You saw a death certificate for her."

"Well … no," I admitted. "But her mother said she was dead."

"Her mother may have been mistaken."

"Maybe. But I don't think so."

Skalaw chuckled again. "You're a remarkable boy. It's easier for you to believe that Draven brought a dead girl to life again rather than to believe that her mother made a mistake? Or maybe it was a lie, a trick, to make you *think* she was brought back to life."

I felt confused. "Maybe it was. I don't know."

"What *do* you know?"

"Not a lot," I confessed. "I only came here a couple of days ago. It's hard to tell because the sun hasn't moved and I don't have a watch."

"You came here from where?"

"Odyssey."

"And where is Odyssey? There's a map here on the wall—"

"It won't be on your map."

"Why not?"

"Because it's in my world."

"Your world?" She looked at me now with a different expression. It was either skepticism or anger, I couldn't tell for certain. "*Your* world as opposed to *our* world?"

I nodded. "That's right. But don't ask me to explain it because I don't know how it happened. One minute I was in a railroad tunnel in Odyssey, and the next minute I was in *this* world. Draven said I'm here because the Unseen One wanted me to come."

"Oh? And why would the Unseen One want you to do that?"

"I'm not sure. To help Draven, I think."

"To help him do what?"

"I don't know yet."

"You really don't know very much, do you?"

I was a little hurt by that remark. "I'm considered smart in Odyssey," I offered in my defense. "My father teaches at the college, and my mother works for the board of education. They've taught me a lot. But no, I don't know what's going on here—any more than you'd know about my world if somebody suddenly dropped you into it."

Skalaw thoughtfully chewed on her bottom lip. I saw her knuckles go white as she clenched the edge of the desk. I thought she might get up and slap me, but her face never lost its composure. Finally she said, "Draven wants to meet with my husband. Why?"

"To talk about starting time again."

"He thinks he has the power to do that?"

"The Unseen One has."

"You believe in the Unseen One?"

"In our world we call Him God, and yeah, I do."

"What would you say if I told you that the Unseen One is a myth and that what has happened to the sun is a temporary glitch of nature?"

"The sun has stood still for over three years and you'd call it a glitch?"

"It has happened before. Millions of years ago. Our scientists have explained it again and again. It's as natural as an eclipse."

"I know a lot about astronomy, but I've never heard of the sun standing still."

"If ever you get the chance, ask my husband's advisers about it," she suggested. "They think they have it all worked out."

"I will," I promised.

She leaned closer on the desk. "Some of us believe there are other forces at work here. Forces greater than the Unseen One. Some of us are empowered by that force."

"Then why don't you unstop the sun?"

"We will when the timing is right."

I frowned. "I thought everyone was miserable. People are sick but can't die, you're running out of food and water, your supreme commander can't even feed his horses. When will the timing be right?"

"When our collective consciousness becomes enlightened," she answered significantly.

"Huh?"

"You see, your Draven friend has it all wrong. There isn't a single god called the Unseen One. There is the accumulation of all beings, all our souls and all our collective power, into one great—"

"Force?" I asked.

"I suppose you could call it a force."

"Does this mean I'll get to meet Luke Skywalker and Obi Wan?" I asked with a smile.

She sighed heavily as she stood up. "I can tell by your tone that you're mocking me." She circled the desk until she was right next to me. I could smell her perfume. Then, faster than I could have imagined, she had my hair in her hand. She yanked my head back quickly and painfully.

"Ouch, ouch, ouch ..." I muttered.

"Don't taunt me, *boy*." She ran a fingernail, long and sharp, across my exposed throat. "I won't be taunted."

"I'm sorry," I said.

She let go of my hair. "How does Draven think he's going to start time again? What trick is he going to pull?"

"He didn't tell me. To be honest, he hasn't told me much of anything."

"And yet you're supposed to help him?"

"That's what he said."

She moved away with her hands clasped behind her back. She wiggled her wrists so that her bracelets jangled. Then she turned to me again. "Many of our ancient texts have written about children from other times and worlds coming to our world to accomplish miracles."

"I heard something about that, too," I offered, now wanting to be as helpful as I could.

"Perhaps *you're* the means by which time will start again," she suggested.

I hadn't thought of that.

"But if you're not around to help Draven, he can't accomplish his trickery." She wasn't talking to me anymore. She was facing the mirror and thinking out loud to whoever watched from the other side. "If we hide this boy away, it might thwart whatever tricks Draven has up his sleeve. Or, since he is from another world, we might be able to kill him."

That was my cue. I sprang from the chair and raced at the hidden panel in the wall. I figured it was better to get lost in those corridors than to hang around and let them hurt me. Unfortunately, the door didn't open. I slammed into it with a hard thud and stumbled back, falling to the floor.

Skalaw laughed. "You stupid boy!"

The bump on my forehead throbbed all over again.

Skalaw went to the regular door and opened it. "I think we should kill him if we can," she announced and walked out. In an instant, several uniformed men came in. The big one called Tesdor grabbed me by the robe and jerked me to my feet.

"I hate killing kids," he said sadly, "but orders is orders."

CHAPTER SEVEN

❖━━━━━━━━❖

"**Y**ou're making a big mistake!" I told the men as they dragged me down the hall.

"Shut up," Tesdor mumbled.

Still shivering from the cold and from fear, I shouted, "But you *can't* kill me!"

Tesdor grunted, "We can try."

We rounded a corner and found ourselves face-to-face with Mobeck, Ladan, and an entourage of guards. "Ah! Just the people we were looking for!" Mobeck exclaimed.

Tesdor dropped me and, along with the other men, saluted. "Supreme Commander!" they said in unison.

"Where are you going with the boy, Tesdor?" Mobeck asked.

"Lady Skalaw has given us instructions to kill the boy," Tesdor replied honestly.

"I think you may have misunderstood her instructions."

"But she said very clearly—"

"*You misunderstood her,*" Mobeck said more firmly.

"Yes, Supreme Commander."

"Go about your business," Mobeck ordered them.

Tesdor tipped his head to the other soldiers, and they turned and marched down the hallway.

Mobeck cast a steely look at Ladan. "And in the future, Ladan," he said sternly, "I suggest you keep a closer eye on your guests."

"Yes, Supreme Commander," Ladan replied, dabbing at his forehead with a handkerchief. "Come along, Scott. It wasn't very polite of you to leave your bath like that."

"But—"

Ladan gave me a hard tug, and we headed away from Mobeck and his guards.

"I don't get it," I said softly as we walked, still shivering.

"Adimah told me that you were missing. I told Mobeck. We both knew Lady Skalaw was behind it."

"But isn't she going to be mad at Mobeck?"

"Mobeck is used to that. The two of them sneak around each other all the time." Ladan gestured to another hall, and we followed it.

"But why would Mobeck protect me?"

"Mobeck wants to have a showdown with Draven, and he's afraid that if you're hurt or locked up, Draven will go back into hiding."

"He *wants* to have a showdown?"

"He's consulted with the greatest scientists of our age. They say that the timing of Draven's challenge is perfect. They say they have the technology to show him up for the fraud he really is."

"Wait a minute!" I said, unsure if I'd heard him right. "They think they know how to start time moving again?"

"Yes."

I shook my head. "But Lady Skalaw thinks it's a natural event, like an eclipse or sunspots or something. She thinks that if everyone collects their conscious-whatevers, they'll start time again."

"I've heard that story before."

We were at the door to Ladan's apartment now. "Lady Skalaw thinks Draven might start time again by using *me* somehow."

"Perhaps he will."

"So you don't know what's going to happen, either?"

"No, I don't." Ladan opened the door and allowed me to go in first. "As you've probably guessed, there's no love lost between Draven and myself."

"Why? You're both believers in the Unseen One."

"True. But we go about our belief in two different ways."

Adimah scurried down the hall toward us. "Thank the Unseen One!" he nearly shouted.

"Let him finish his bath, but *stay with him* this time," Ladan commanded. "And put some kind of lock on that secret panel. I'm tired of people coming in and out whenever they want."

Adimah bowed slightly and led me back to the bathtub. He'd obviously topped it off with hot water, and I slid in with the same sense of warmth and comfort as I'd had before. It was a relief after everything that had happened.

Afterward, Adimah presented me with my own clothes, cleaned and dried. When I had dressed, he took me into a small dining room, where I ate silently with Ladan. Then Adimah took me back to the guest bedroom and laid out some pajamas for me to wear. When I was snug in bed, he sat down in a nearby chair. His body was tense, as if he expected someone to try to nab me again. I could hear Ladan pacing back and forth in the hall.

"He's a pretty nervous guy," I observed about Ladan.

"I'd be nervous, too, if I were in his shoes," Adimah said. "He's under a lot of pressure. Imagine being the only recognized priest for the Unseen One in this country."

"But what good is it if he's under Mobeck's thumb?"

Adimah was instantly indignant. "Who told you that?" he demanded.

"It was the impression I got," I replied sheepishly.

Adimah snorted. "Draven thinks everyone should be a

radical like he is. He believes challenge and confrontation are the only way to deal with Mobeck."

"Ladan doesn't?"

"Ladan works from *within* the system, influencing Mobeck from here. Ladan is not what he appears to be. He's a courageous man."

"Really?"

Adimah leaned closer to the bed and said in a half whisper, "A few years ago, before Draven came along, Lady Skalaw argued that speaking out on behalf of the Unseen One was a crime against the state. She decided to purge the country of anyone who professed to be a voice for Him. Hundreds of people were in danger. But Ladan, at great risk, helped them to secretly escape and hide. They are alive and safe to this day because of Ladan. That's how he works. And though it's different from Draven's approach, both have their places in the work of the Unseen One. I believe, in fact, that Draven is alive today because Ladan reminds Mobeck of his dormant faith."

I didn't know how to respond, so I lay quietly. Soon I was asleep. If I had any dreams, I didn't remember them the next day.

Morning came with Adimah waking me for a breakfast of powdered eggs and toast that tasted like cardboard. After that, there was a chaotic scramble as Ladan got ready for us to leave. He didn't know if the occasion called for his usual suit or his priestly robes. He finally decided on his suit. And then there was a question about which car he and I would ride in, Mobeck's or one of the cars that would follow. Eventually it was all sorted out and we got into Mobeck's limousine in front of the palace.

"Did you sleep well?" Mobeck asked me.

I said that I had.

"Good."

"Where is Lady Skalaw?" Ladan asked.

Mobeck smiled. "I persuaded my wife to leave this particular meeting to me."

We drove out of Sarum and followed a major highway toward Hailsham. Fields and villages zoomed past, and after about 20 minutes, we came to a gate with a sign saying, "The Field of the Great Kings." A small road wound through the park, taking us past vast lawns, an occasional statue, fields with grazing deer—"Royal deer," Mobeck explained, "so it's a crime to kill them"—and then into a deeply wooded area. We stopped and got out, and only then did I realize that all the cars that had been following us had disappeared.

"Maiden's Bridge is that way," the driver informed Mobeck, pointing.

Mobeck glanced at his watch. "Ten o'clock. Right on time."

We followed a dirt path farther into the woods. Maiden's Bridge was a small, wooden bridge that sat over what had been a stream but was now a dry bed. Several large oak trees, their fat branches bare, stood over us.

Mobeck, Ladan, and I walked to the center of the bridge and stopped. Mobeck leaned against the railing and looked around casually. I wondered if he were up to something. What had become of all those other cars following us? Was he planning a trick or a trap for Draven? I glanced at Ladan. As usual, he was nervously patting his forehead with his handkerchief.

"I'm glad you could make it," we suddenly heard Draven say.

Startled, the three of us turned around on the bridge to look for him, but he wasn't anywhere we could see.

"Is that the troublemaker?" Mobeck called out.

"You started the trouble when you compromised your faith in the Unseen One," Draven said.

"Where are you?" Mobeck asked.

Draven laughed. "I haven't come all this way to be tricked by your feeble plan. I know the park is surrounded by your soldiers. Are they under orders to shoot me or to take me alive?"

"Take you alive, of course," Mobeck admitted. "You're no good to me dead."

"I'm no good to you alive, either," Draven countered.

"Then come out and say what you have to say." Mobeck was now looking around the bridge, leaning over the rail to see if Draven were underneath. Instead he found a speaker lodged into the woodwork. With brute force, he pulled it out and held it up for us to see.

"That's right," Draven said. "I'm broadcasting my voice."

Mobeck held the speaker up even higher. "But you can see me, can't you?" he asked. "You're somewhere nearby."

"Maybe I am, and maybe I'm watching you by other means. But we're not going to get very far in our conversation at this pace. Send your guards away or I'll leave you now, and time will remain just as it is."

Mobeck pounded his fist against the rail angrily. "By the two moons! You're going to dictate terms to *me*?"

"Yep."

Mobeck thought about it for a moment, then held up his hand, circled his finger in the air, and jerked his thumb. Whatever he meant by the signal, suddenly soldiers appeared from behind trees and moved away. I heard car engines start in the distance and the sound of tires spinning on gravel. Everyone was leaving.

"Are you satisfied?" Mobeck asked Draven.

"Thank you," he replied.

"Now tell me what you want."

"I want to meet you and all your so-called advisers tomorrow at noon at the University of Hailsham."

"Oh, you do, do you?"

"Yes. You may even bring all of Skalaw's pagan priests. And I want you to bring all the national radio and television networks."

"That's quite a tall order. I don't know if I can assemble everyone in such a short time."

"Nonsense. Most of them came to Sarum for your banquet last night."

Mobeck chuckled. "And why should I bring everyone to meet you?"

"Because you want time to start moving again."

"And how do I know you can do that?" Mobeck asked.

"You don't. But in front of the entire nation, I'm going to challenge all your best minds—your scientists and technicians and even your wife's bogus priests—to try to release time. And when they can't, the Unseen One will."

"I see. You're challenging us to a contest."

"Exactly," Draven agreed. "And don't be so boring as to try any tricks to catch me in the meantime."

Mobeck hesitated, then said, "All right, I won't. Is there anything else you want from me?"

"You and Ladan should walk to your car without looking back," Draven instructed.

"What about the boy?"

"Leave him here on the bridge."

"If you insist." Mobeck spun on his heel and strode off the bridge.

"Draven," Ladan suddenly called out.

"Yes?"

"Is there anything you want *me* to do?"

"Yes," he answered. "Try to keep out of the way."

Ladan turned a bright red and stormed off toward the car. I glanced around, wondering what would happen next.

Mobeck and Ladan were nearly out of sight down the path. Suddenly a loop of rope fell down from above me.

"Grab on," Draven said softly.

I put my arm through the loop and was pulled far up into the thick branches of the oak tree. I hadn't realized how big they were, but obviously they were large enough for Draven to sit up there without being seen, because there he was at the other end of the rope.

"Watch," Draven whispered and pointed toward a clearing through the branches. Ladan was just getting into the limousine. But Mobeck couldn't resist one last look and turned to see if I were still on the bridge. He squinted and craned his neck. Then, when he saw I had gone, his mouth fell open and he looked quickly around. It didn't seem to occur to him to look up. If he had, he might have seen the two of us smiling at him. Clearly annoyed, Mobeck got into the limousine, and it sped away.

"Let's relax for a few minutes, just to make sure they leave the park," Draven said, lying back into the crook of two branches with his hands behind his head.

"Why didn't Mobeck or his men think to look for you in the trees?" I wondered aloud.

"Because it's too simple," Draven said sarcastically. "The simple things are too much for a mind like Mobeck's to cope with. He expects some cunning trickery or a complicated scheme."

"I guess that explains why he thinks it's easier to believe in science and technology than to believe in the Unseen One," I offered.

"I suppose so."

We waited in the tree for about a half hour, and then Draven signaled for me to follow him. We crawled across from one branch to another, and then from tree to tree, until I couldn't see the bridge anymore.

"I used to do this when I was a boy," he said happily.

Then, like a couple of squirrels, we scurried down to the ground. We were in front of a small caretaker's shed, which was made out of cinder blocks and had an iron door. Draven pulled open the door, and we went inside. It was jammed with equipment for the park—a lawn mower, rakes, shovels, tools, and the like. In the center of the floor was a grate. Draven lifted it.

"A tunnel?" I asked.

Draven nodded. "You go first. There's a long ladder attached to the wall. Climb down and wait at the bottom. Don't mind the dark—or the rats."

"Rats?" I gulped.

"They don't bite," he said, smiling. "They only nibble."

With a shiver, I made my way down the ladder and stayed as close to the small shaft of light from above as I could. Draven followed, pausing only to put the grate back in place.

Joining me at the bottom, he produced a small flashlight from his jacket pocket. He turned it on and pointed it ahead of us into the drainage tunnel. "Be careful of the puddles," he advised.

We walked through a maze of tunnels—I never saw a single rat, by the way—and eventually came out into the open air again at the edge of the park. A motorcycle was leaning against a wall.

"This is yours?" I asked.

Draven handed me a helmet and put on one of his own. "Climb on," he said.

"Cool."

We buzzed down the highway to the small village called

Hailsham. It contained shops and restaurants that looked tailored for the young, smart students from the nearby university. Men in black-and-red uniforms and suits of the same colors milled around. Women in sharp outfits of red tops and black skirts joined them. We passed by an ornate railroad station that stood in the middle of the village like a proud dog. On the outskirts of Hailsham, we came to a road with a lot of ruts and potholes. I had to hang on tight for fear I might bounce off the back of the motorcycle.

At the end of the road sat a run-down cottage covered with vines. "This is the place," Draven said as we climbed off the motorcycle. "We'll stay here until our big showdown tomorrow."

I looked around. The house sat near brown hills and an overgrown patch of trees that looked out onto a valley. Through the thicket, I could make out Hailsham in the center of the valley, and beyond that was an impressive collection of buildings I hadn't seen from the road. "What are those?" I asked, pointing.

"The grand and prestigious University of Hailsham," Draven replied derisively. "Once upon a time, in the days of Arin, Hailsham was the center of all that was supposed to be right and good about Marus. Weapons of mass destruction were created there, only to be undone by the Unseen One and leveled to the ground. For years this was beautiful countryside once again. But since the rise of Mobeck, it has become the largest education center in West Marus, spouting the supposed wisdom and advancements of the age. It's the perfect venue for this final showdown." He paused as a smile crept across his face. "Besides, it has the largest clock in the nation."

The cottage had a thatched roof and, where I could see through the thick vines, was mostly white. It had dark, vertical beams of timber that ran from the roof to the ground and shut-tered windows. It made me think of a picture I'd once seen of a Tudor cottage in England.

Then something dawned on me. "They're green!" I said to Draven, pointing to the vines. "Is this cottage outside time, too?"

Draven nodded, then paused at the cottage door and said like a prayer, "May we always remember the Old Judge's strength." He patted the wooden door frame affectionately and then lifted the latch on the thick, oak door and pushed it open.

Dust sprayed over us as Draven shoved aside the curtains and threw open the windows and shutters. A damp chill filled my bones. Shelves and paintings hung cockeyed from the dark, paneled walls. A fireplace nearly filled one wall, and two patched-up chairs sat on a faded carpet. A large hutch sat off to the side, but whatever had once filled its shelves was long gone. I was surprised to see a grandfather clock in the corner. I was even more surprised to see that it was still working, its arm swinging back and forth. I assumed that Draven often stayed here and wound the clock himself.

A second room contained a sink, a stove, and some cup-boards. I saw a large bed through one doorway and a smaller one through a second doorway, and a third door was closed.

"Is this your cottage?" I asked. "Is that why it's outside time?"

Draven went into the kitchen and filled a kettle with some water. "This cottage once belonged to a great voice of the Unseen One," he explained. "He was called the Old Judge. He was influential in the reign of King Lawrence and the rise of Darien, our greatest king."

"Marus has a pretty long history."

"Thousands of years."

"I like history. Do you have any books I can read about it?"

"You can check in there," Draven said, nodding toward the closed door.

The room was packed with buckling shelves of books, old boxes, and trunks filled with clothes. The mustiness made me cough, but the books, with their leather bindings and gold-leaf lettering, made me feel as if I'd come upon a giant treasure. I had fallen in love with reading because of my parents, so I couldn't help but think of them now. They would have drooled over this room.

I found one book whose title claimed to give an account of the history of Marus and took it back into the living room.

"Did you find anything?" Draven asked from the kitchen. From the sound of it, he was making us lunch.

"This one," I answered, holding up the book. "It's called *A Concise History of Marus: From Its Beginnings to the Present Time*." I flipped to the back of the book. "It looks like it goes to the time of Darien's rule as king."

"That's a couple of hundred years ago. But reading up to that point should keep you busy."

So I began to read. And there, in short, terse sentences, was the amazing history of the nation of Marus. It began with the creation of all the world by the Unseen One and the story of how the original man and the original woman were duped by a serpent in a tree and ousted from paradise. I read about the stretch of years after that which led up to an age of true knowledge, when it seemed as if mankind had reached a pinnacle—only to allow wickedness and a denial of the Unseen One to lead them to self-worship. This period should have been glorious, but it became the Age of Apostasy. The Unseen One sent a man called Arin, His voice—what we would call a prophet in our world, I realized—to beg the nation to repent. But the people refused. Then came a mysterious boy, sent by the Unseen One from another world, to bring judgment and destruction to Marus. Only Arin and his family were saved. The book didn't say what happened to the boy.

Draven gave me a sandwich of something that tasted like roast beef and some vegetables, and he didn't seem to mind that I wanted to keep reading while I ate.

A man named Marus was called by the Unseen One to establish a nation of true believers. Another "mystery child" came to help him with his travels to what would become the capital city of Sarum. I then learned that *Sarum* is a slight variation on "Marus" spelled backward and was so named because Marus had doubted the Unseen One and did the opposite of what he'd been told to do when moving into the land.

There were stories of the growth of Marus and the years when its leaders did not lead or did not obey the Unseen One and chaos ensued. Out of the chaos came new people of faith, including a young man named Glennall who was betrayed by his own family and sold into slavery, but who rose to power with the help of yet another mysterious child from another world.

"This is the story of Joseph!" I said, growing excited at the connection. "This is just like a story from our Bible."

"Your what?" Draven asked.

"The Bible! It's the book that tells the story of God and a nation called Israel."

Draven nodded thoughtfully. "Then the Unseen One is working in your world, too."

"Yeah!" I said, then thought about it. "But why would He do the same things in this world as He did in ours? I mean, it's one thing to have parallel worlds, but to have the same kinds of things happen in them seems a little strange."

Draven shrugged. "Maybe it has more to do with the flaws of creation than with the Unseen One—just as a doctor may have to treat similar diseases in similar ways but in different parts of the world."

I shook my head, puzzled.

Draven turned to the window. "I'm not inclined to second-guess the Unseen One, but some of our great philosophers have suggested some theories. Berlion, whose books of wisdom are included in our Sacred Scrolls, wrote that time, space, and the existence of other worlds and dimensions are to be expected in a vast creation. He said, and I quote, 'We exist in the same pool, with events rippling back and forth between us, our reflections dancing in the water as pale imitations of the full truth of the Unseen One and His purposes. And as long as we remain under the watchful eye of the Unseen One, who is God of all realms and all worlds, then we may live in a full faith, in harmony with the unknown. For we are *all* in the care of the Unseen One.'"

I thought about what he had said for a while, but I couldn't decide whether I agreed with it. I'm not even sure I understood it. But it *sounded* good, so I went back to the book. I read about how three mysterious children had brought about the signs that helped the great deliverer Fendar lead the Marutians from slavery and back to Marus.

"Why don't they ever say their names?" I impatiently asked Draven, who was still looking out the window.

"Whose names?"

"The names of the children who came from other worlds to help your people."

He shrugged. "I was taught that the names of the children were never to be spoken for fear that the people would honor them over the Unseen One who had brought them." Then he added, "But the names are known among the voices of the Unseen One."

"Then what were the names of the children who helped Fendar?"

Draven turned to me and said with a smile, "I said the names are known among the *voices* of the Unseen One. You are not a voice yet, are you?"

"But it's not fair," I complained. "I'll bet some of these kids are from *my* world. I might even know who they are!"

Draven smiled again. "You'll have to be patient."

I returned to the history book. Confusion continued as the people of Marus vacillated between belief and unbelief in the Unseen One, even as His leaders gave them the length and breadth of Marus. Another child assisted Emit as he conquered parts of the land. Still other children came at crucial points when it seemed as if all were lost. Neighboring countries took advantage of Marus's internal squabbles and invaded, but heroes arose to fight them. There was Chantall in the south, who battled with the Palatians. There was also Fletcher in the north, who, with the help of a girl and a boy from another world, drove out their oppressors. Then came the Old Judge and King Lawrence and a brother and a sister—a protector and a voice—who helped Darien rise to power.

I closed the book. According to the clock, it was now early evening. Draven hadn't moved from his place at the window.

I wanted to ask Draven what had happened in Marus after Darien, but he looked as if he were contemplating the secrets of the universe. "Is something wrong?" I asked instead.

Draven continued to gaze out the window, and his voice took on a soft, deliberate tone. "Some of the voices have spoken about the mystery of a great sacrifice, one which shattered the boundaries of time and space. It was a single act by a single man that will eventually bring all worlds together under one faith. Mathan, a voice of old, called it the Final Victory."

"Wait a minute, you said that like it's already happened."

"It has."

"When? Is it in this book?"

"No. It has happened, but it hasn't been revealed to us. Mathan, who some believed could see into the future, wrote that the Unseen One will reveal the Final Victory when He thinks the time is right. Meanwhile, we have to wait."

I took a deep breath of excitement as I suddenly realized what the great sacrifice was. "I think I know what it is, Draven," I told him.

He turned to me, a sad expression on his face. "I suspect that you do. I suspect that all the children from your world have known."

"Do you want me to tell you?"

"No," he replied. "The Unseen One will tell us when He's ready—when *we're* ready."

"But I could tell you now."

"No! Don't you see? Telling me now, before the right time, could be catastrophic. It could bring untold disaster on all of us." He shoved his hands deep into his jacket pockets and frowned. "Our purpose is to play out our parts in *this* time, in *this* place, to the best of our abilities. The future belongs to the Unseen One. Now, don't say any more. We have a job to do." He strode across the floor and out the front door. I went to the window and watched him walk toward the fields. His shoulders shook as he walked. I wondered if he was crying.

He didn't return until later that night, after I'd crawled into the smaller bed. I heard him pacing the floor. Then he went to bed, too.

I thought about the pacing. Draven had done it just as

Ladan had the night before. And then it occurred to me that they hadn't been pacing only. They had been praying.

Is he worried about tomorrow? I wondered. *Maybe he's nervous that something will go wrong.*

I sure would be, I concluded as I stared at the ceiling the rest of the night.

CHAPTER EIGHT

At 11 the next morning, we walked across the fields toward Hailsham and the university. I felt woozy from my lack of sleep the night before, or maybe I was nervous with excitement. Draven walked with a grim determination on his face.

The University of Hailsham was a collection of large buildings embellished with crests, statues, and comical-looking gargoyles that sat hunched over the rooftops and watched us with leering smiles. In the center sat the main administrative building with its high tower, and in the tower was the clock Draven had mentioned to me. It was gigantic. I noticed that its hands were at stopped at 7:04.

"Why isn't the clock working?" I asked Draven.

"It's a specially designed solar clock," he replied. "It stopped when the sun stopped."

Mobeck's people had been hard at work since yesterday. Scaffolding had been erected as a temporary stage in front of the clock, with hundreds of seats positioned on the broad mall in front of that. Technicians were busy setting up microphones, loudspeakers, and cameras. People turned to us as we approached, whispering and pointing. We stopped at the edge of the main stage.

"I want you to find a seat here," Draven said to me. "If anything goes wrong, run for your life."

"Can something go wrong?" I asked in surprise.

Draven smiled. "Something can *always* go wrong." Then he went over to a guard at the foot of the stage. "I'm Draven," I heard him say.

The guard nodded. "Follow me," he instructed.

They walked up a set of makeshift stairs to the top of the stage. The guard showed Draven to a seat and then asked him a few questions that Draven answered by shaking his head yes or no. After the guard left, Draven waited calmly and patiently, watching the workers add the final touches of artificial plants and decorative banners to the stage.

Eventually a small brass band came and set up in a semi-circle of chairs on the other side of the stage. People arrived for the showdown, and before I had realized it, the hundreds of seats behind me were filled. Those who couldn't find seats crowded in around the sides and at the back. Some country folk had brought in horse-drawn wagons and allowed people to sit in them for a clearer view.

The leader of the band received a cue from somewhere and suddenly waved his baton at the players. They struck up a tune I'd never heard before, but it must have been some kind of formal theme because everyone stood up. A procession of people dressed in academic robes marched down the long steps of the main university building. I figured they must be Mobeck's advisers. On and on they came, at least a couple hundred of them, and took their seats along the back of the stage, passing Draven along the way. One or two of them even tried to talk to him. Draven ignored them.

I looked for Ladan but couldn't see him in the sea of faces.

Then Mobeck came, waving to the crowd, whose members now applauded wildly, whistled, and shouted their appreciation. He strode up the steps of the stage and went straight to the microphone. The television cameras quickly focused on him. The band stopped playing, and everyone sat down.

"My fellow citizens—great Marutians all!" he shouted.

All the people leaped to their feet again and applauded.

He waved them down. "It is in the spirit of goodwill and tolerance that I welcome you all here today." He turned to one of the cameras and added, "And I welcome our listening and viewing audience as well. What a glorious day!"

The audience cheered, and I wondered what could be glorious about the day, since it was the same day they'd been experiencing for the past three years.

"My wife sends her regards," Mobeck went on. At the mention of Lady Skalaw, more cheers came. "She has less patience with the antics of our special guest, so she stayed at the palace with her advisers." Mobeck turned toward Draven. "I ask you. Where else in the world would the supreme commander and his entire government gather at the request of an ordinary citizen?" Mobeck then forced a chuckle. "No, I correct myself. He is not an ordinary citizen. He is Draven, whom I affectionately call my *troublemaker*."

The crowd jeered and booed Draven.

Mobeck held up his hands in mock rebuke. "Now, now, none of that. Draven means well, I'm sure. He is a victim of a rigid upbringing, having been brainwashed from an early age to believe in old superstitions."

The crowd laughed now. Draven sat in stony silence, his legs crossed casually, his hands cradling his knee. His face betrayed no emotion.

"But he demanded that we meet together today to hear him once more. And I've graciously obliged," Mobeck said, then turned to Draven. "The microphone is yours, my *troublemaker*."

The crowd applauded as Mobeck went to his chair and sat down. Draven stood up and walked purposefully to the front of the stage. He adjusted the microphone to his height—he was taller than Mobeck—and gently cleared his throat. He spoke in a low, clear voice that seemed to penetrate the very walls surrounding us.

"People of Marus, how long will you waver in your faith in the Unseen One? The choice is clear. You can follow Mobeck and Skalaw to your destruction, or you can follow the Unseen One to salvation. Which will it be?"

The crowd was still.

"I am the one voice of the Unseen One remaining, but Mobeck has *hundreds* of advisers. Look at them! The brightest and the best of Marus, or so Mobeck claims. Yet for over three years they have been unable to undo what the Unseen One accomplished with a flick of His finger. By His word, the sun stopped in the sky so that you would know His power and understand the consequences of your infidelity."

He paused for a moment. I could feel the crowd move in their seats.

"Today is the day of reckoning!" Draven exclaimed and pointed at the large clock. "I challenge Mobeck and all his advisers to now prove their worth. If they can start that clock again, they deserve to be followed by the entire world and I will retreat, never bothering you again."

The audience applauded this statement.

"But," Draven continued sharply, "if they cannot move the hands of this clock by restoring time, you will witness today the terrifying power of the Unseen One. Choose whom you will believe!"

Draven returned to his chair and sat down.

Mobeck stood up, bowed formally to Draven, then went to the microphone. He had to adjust it down again, then said, "As usual, my advisers were more than happy to rise to this challenge. For they have not been idle for the past three years but have been working day and night to study, explore, and come to understand this event. To begin, I'd like to introduce Dr. Quartis, the head of a team that has focused on the psychological ramifications. Dr. Quartis?"

A short man with thick, red hair and a scraggly beard came forward.

"Explain your theory to them, please," Mobeck said.

Dr. Quartis blew into the microphone a couple of times to make sure it was working. "Greetings, everyone," he began. "My colleagues and I have been considering the unique nature of our problem. We asked ourselves, has the sun truly stopped in the sky or has something *else* happened? Is it possible that reality itself has not changed but that our *perception* of reality has?"

"The hands of the clock are not moving!" Draven called out to the doctor.

Dr. Quartis continued, "Some of us believe that three years ago, this man Draven, with the help of foreign agents, infected our water supplies with a special hypnotic drug. At the time, we were alarmed to discover traces of it in the streams, in our water tanks, and in our water recycling centers. With that drug, Draven was able to facilitate mass hypnosis."

Titters and laughter spread out around the crowd. "Are you saying we've been *hypnotized* for the past three years?" someone shouted. "Everyone in the world has been hypnotized?"

Dr. Quartis waved his hands at them. "Hear me out! We have proof, evidence of this diabolical scheme! Draven and his accomplices have created mass hysteria through drugs and hypnotism!"

Draven cupped his hands around his mouth and shouted again, "The hands of the clock are still not moving!"

Some of the crowd laughed, and others began to hoot and holler at Dr. Quartis.

Undaunted, he reached into the pocket of his robe and pulled out a small bottle. "We have produced an antidote. If everyone would drink this and embark on a nationwide course of therapy, we will correct our perceptions of reality! And then you will see that the sun has been rising and setting as it always has!"

The abuse from the crowd turned into an uproar. Dr. Quartis pleaded with them to let him speak further. Mobeck, seeing that the doctor had lost his audience, went up to him and persuaded him to sit down again. He motioned the audience to be quiet.

"Is that the best you can do?" Draven asked when the crowd had calmed down.

Mobeck answered, "It is a mark of our open-mindedness that we have explored all possibilities. I have found Dr. Quartis's theories interesting and helpful. Do me the courtesy of refraining from childish behavior or my guards will dismiss this audience."

The people, knowing a threat when they heard one, went completely still.

"Now I would like us to listen to one of Marus's most-eminent astronomers, Dr. Probam," Mobeck said sternly.

A slender man with thick glasses, a wiry smile, and short, gray hair came to the microphone. "Thank you, Supreme Commander," he started. He shoved his hands into his robe pockets and looked like a college instructor addressing a classroom of students. "Those of us who study the stars have been considering the many planetary configurations of the past three years. The universe, as you know, is a vast mechanism, not unlike a clock—"

"Speaking of *clocks*," Draven interrupted and hooked a thumb at the large solar clock.

"Draven, please," Dr. Probam complained. "Professional respect, if you don't mind."

"I don't think you're a professional, nor do you deserve respect," Draven said.

Dr. Probam ignored him. "I'll come straight to the point. It is the considered opinion of the world's leading astronomers that what has happened with the sun is a purely natural phenomenon. It is part of the cycle of the universe, no different from the passing of the seasons, that once every few thousand years, the rotation of the earth slows down to what seems to us a complete stop. We have records dating to the pre-Catastrophic Era that show that—"

Draven yawned loudly in an exaggerated manner and turned to look at the clock again.

Dr. Probam lost his patience. "Listen to me, you charlatan! We know your tricks. You tell us that the Unseen One will restore time, but *we* say that time will restore itself!"

"Oh, really?" Draven asked. "When?"

"By our calculations, the earth will resume its rotation in another 14 years."

"Fourteen years!" many in the audience cried.

"Yes! And then you'll see that it has nothing to do with nonsense about judgmental gods or ancient deities!" Dr. Probam turned to Draven again, his face red with anger. "And if it were up to me, you'd be publicly executed right here and now!"

Mobeck approached Dr. Probam and whispered something in his ear. The doctor nodded and sat down. Mobeck sidled up to the microphone again. "Thank you, Dr. Probam," he said, casting a steely gaze at the unruly members of the crowd.

"You're stalling, Mobeck," Draven challenged. "The hands of the clock have still not moved."

Mobeck smiled cruelly, and for the first time I saw how much his face resembled a wolf's. "You taunt us, but you'll soon regret your words," he returned.

Draven lifted his eyebrows as if to say, "Will I?"

"Marutians!" Mobeck shouted dramatically. "I allowed Dr. Quartis and Dr. Probam to speak to you as a prelude to this next gentleman. He is considered by all to be the greatest mind of our age, and he has not only sorted out the problem, but also created a solution! Dr. Balama!"

The crowd erupted in frenzied applause. I searched the seats of robed advisers to see who would stand, but no one did. Then I realized that he hadn't come in with the rest. A tall man with a burst of white hair and a long, white beard walked slowly from the main university building. He descended the stairs, circled the stage, and joined Mobeck at the microphone. He looked terribly uncomfortable about being there and waved a hand at the audience as if hoping they would calm down or go away.

Mobeck adjusted the microphone for him and took a couple of steps back.

Dr. Balama looked shyly at the audience for a moment, his cheeks red from embarrassment. Finally, the people grew quiet.

"Ladies and gentlemen," Dr. Balama said in a voice soft and earnest, "we—I mean the scientists and advisers assembled here—have taken seriously the task put before us. Time has stopped, and we must start it again. For over three years we have studied the problem. We took to heart Dr. Quartis's theories about mass hypnotism and agree that our *friend* Draven and other conspirators used artificial means to bring fear to our hearts. We agree with Dr. Probam that this is nothing more than a natural phenomenon, one which Draven and his fellow traitors knew about and exploited by attributing it to the judgment of the Unseen One."

He paused to touch a handkerchief to his lips, then continued, "Men in times past have done the same. In days of old, men claimed that the Unseen One had judged our world and destroyed it through the words of Arin. We now know that an unknown virus, one to which they had no resistance or immunity, destroyed that world. So you see? It was a natural phenomenon that unscrupulous men used to promote their outdated faith."

I looked at Draven, wondering what he was thinking about this quiet attack on him. For a second we made eye contact, and he winked at me.

Dr. Balama went on. "The difference between then and now is that we have the intelligence, the skill, and the resources to refute the old ways of thinking. This natural phenomenon"— here he waved his hand at the clock—"may well take 14 years to undo itself. But we do not have the patience for that. We must take the course of events, our *destiny*, into our own hands."

Draven sat up impatiently. "I hope the hands of that clock start moving faster than your hands!" he said.

Dr. Balama giggled. "They will move, dear Draven," he replied. "They will move."

"Tell them how," Mobeck interjected.

"Our scientists and technicians have been working for the past two years on explosives, bombs which are so powerful that just *one* of them is greater than all the bombs of history put together." Dr. Balama clasped his hands behind his back and waited.

A hush fell over the crowd. No one moved. I'm not sure anyone was breathing. I wondered if this meant that the scientists of Marus had created an atomic bomb or a hydrogen bomb or maybe something even more powerful. Suddenly I was worried.

"Tell them what these bombs will do," Mobeck encouraged the doctor.

"Ah!" he said and held up a bony finger. "We have drilled deep into the earth, in strategic places all over the world—"

"In those countries we're allied with," Mobeck interjected.

"Yes," Dr. Balama said, "and we have put our bombs there. Deep in the earth. And when we explode those bombs, all together at exactly the same time, the rotation of the earth will begin again."

I shook my head, unsure if I had heard what I'd just heard. They were going to *jolt* the earth back into its rotation? Obviously the audience also wondered and began whispering among themselves.

Dr. Balama continued to explain, "We have tested this theory in our laboratory, using the latest technology. The bombs will explode so deeply underground and away from populated areas that no one will be hurt."

Mobeck was smiling again. "When can we do this, Dr. Balama?" he asked, obviously knowing the answer already.

Dr. Balama shrugged. "We are prepared to do it right now," he said casually.

It took a moment for the reality of what he'd said to sink in. Then, like a wave, a buzz went through the audience.

"Thank you, doctor," Mobeck said and took charge of the microphone again. "Ladies and gentlemen, Draven asked us to come together to witness the power of the Unseen One. Well, we've fooled him. We have come together to witness the power of Marutian intelligence and technology over nature itself!" He signaled somebody offstage. "As supreme commander, I order the technicians around the world to prepare the detonators! Bring me the radio activator!"

Is this possible? I wondered, clenching and unclenching my fists nervously.

A soldier came onto the stage with a large box. He set it at Mobeck's feet and then raised an antenna from the back. A thin wire was attached to a smaller box, which the soldier handed to Mobeck.

Mobeck held up the small box. There was a bright-red button on it. "I will push this, and then the world will know!" he declared. He then lifted his hand to the side of his head, and I realized he was wearing some kind of earpiece. "Are we ready?" he asked someone we couldn't see. "Yes, the reports are coming in from all stations," he told the crowd. "All systems are go!"

Draven sat impassively. I wondered if he realized what would happen to him—and to me—if this crazy scheme somehow worked.

With great drama, Mobeck announced, "Ladies and gentlemen, fellow Marutians, viewers from around the world, I give you *time!*"

He pushed the button.

CHAPTER NINE

At first I wasn't sure I heard anything at all, because the sound of muffled explosions was so soft. It might have been the roar of a distant ocean wave for all I knew. But then the sound came closer, as if a huge truck were driving past the campus. I thought I felt the ground shake beneath me—or it might have been my knees knocking together.

The sound subsided, and everyone sat in wonder. I looked up at the clock. The hands hadn't moved.

It might have been a minute, maybe two, and then everyone started to get restless. Nothing was happening.

"Be patient," Dr. Balama appealed to the crowd. "It will not happen in an instant."

So we waited, every eye fixed on the hands of the giant clock.

After another five minutes or so, Draven said, "Maybe you need a little more gunpowder in those bombs."

"Don't be ridiculous," Dr. Balama snapped.

The wait continued. Mobeck pressed his hand against his earpiece and said excitedly, "I'm getting a report from Anadia in the far west. Something is happening. Something ..."

But whatever it was must have stopped, because Mobeck lowered his head. "One of the explosions triggered a small earthquake there," he reported softly.

"At least you got *something* to move," Draven teased. "But the hands on that clock are exactly where they were."

"Do something!" Mobeck snarled at Dr. Balama angrily, then went to his chair and sat down. Dr. Balama shrugged helplessly. Mobeck folded his arms across his chest and pouted like a little boy.

Draven stood up and addressed the advisers. "Is there anyone else? Do we have any other volunteers to embarrass themselves?"

As if in answer, an odd commotion arose behind the stage, out of sight. First there was a low *thump, thump* of someone hitting a drum, followed by the shaking of tambourines and a strange chanting. Then I saw Lady Skalaw, dressed in a brightly colored robe, her hair adorned with artificial flowers, march in and around the stage. She was followed by her advisers, men and women, also dressed in brightly colored robes.

"By the two moons!" Mobeck exclaimed and stood up.

Draven watched them come with a smirk on his face. "The show goes on," he said and sat down again.

Lady Skalaw went up on the stage with her entourage, forcing Mobeck and his advisers to move back. Draven refused to budge.

"What are you doing?" Mobeck asked his wife.

"I have been watching this charade with the deepest humiliation," she said into the microphone. "The time has come for the truth to be seen. The people are ready for an end to their suffering and confusion."

The crowd, shaken from their boredom, now applauded her.

"Together we will shake the forces of nature!" she proclaimed. "Everyone here—and everyone watching and listening from their homes—may now join with me, uniting our wills, combining our spirits, and then the earth will move, the sun will slide through the sky as it once did, and the hands on the clock shall turn in harmony with us! Are you ready?" she shouted.

The crowd didn't know how to answer. A few said yes.

Not satisfied with such a feeble response, she shouted again, "Are you ready?"

More in the crowd shouted back, "Yes!"

"We must do this together!" she demanded. "If we will it, if we channel the energy of our collective life force, we will move the world! Will you join with me or not?"

The crowd, getting more excited, said they would.

"Then say it!" she cried. "Say it to the heavens! Say you are ready!"

"We are ready!" the audience called out.

Then the drums and tambourines began a steady, rhythmic beat, and Skalaw and her advisers began to dance on the stage. The beat intensified, and some of the advisers fell onto the stage, writhing and screaming, with their hands and arms waving wildly.

"I can't *feel* you!" Skalaw shouted at the crowd. "I can't feel your energy!"

Some of the audience began to dance now, waving their arms and kicking their legs in the air.

Draven sat where he was, looking unimpressed. From the looks of it, Mobeck wasn't terribly impressed, either.

Skalaw beckoned the drummers and tambourine players to increase the tempo, building it and building it as her advisers and many in the audience worked themselves into a frenzy.

"Channel your energy to me!" she begged. "Give me your power! We will move the hands of time!"

The frenzy continued until people collapsed from exhaustion.

Draven looked up at the clock. "The reception on your channels must not be very good," he jeered. "The clock isn't moving."

Skalaw beckoned to the crowd to try harder, to concentrate, and to pray. Again the drums beat and the tambourines shook, and everyone was whipped into a new frenzy.

Nothing happened.

But Skalaw wouldn't give up. The afternoon wore on with her shouts at the audience, the wild dancing, and the cry for a collective power that wouldn't come. In their deranged movements, her advisers suddenly brought out knives and began to cut their arms.

"We will let our life force free!" they screamed.

Draven watched them and began to laugh. It was a chuckle at first, and then he laughed loud and heartily. The harder Skalaw and her advisers tried to "channel" their energy, the funnier he found it all.

Finally, when everyone had reached a point of total exhaustion, Mobeck went to Skalaw and begged her to go home. "It's no use, my dear," he said.

"No," she gasped. "We can make it happen!"

"You'll make it happen or you'll all bleed to death," Draven mocked.

Skalaw drew a knife from a sheath in her waistband and lunged at Draven with an angry cry. Mobeck intercepted her just in time, catching her arms and pulling her back. She collapsed wearily to the floor of the stage. Mobeck signaled his soldiers. "Take her home," he ordered them. She went along without resistance. Her advisers slowly crawled to the rear of the stage.

Draven moved to the microphone. His moment had come.

"Mobeck, you and your stooges and your paid liars have been seen for what you truly are," he declared. "Today is the day of choice. The people must decide whom they will follow. They have now seen the work of your doctors and scientists.

They have witnessed the foolishness of Skalaw's false religion. The power of man is nothing. Marus will only be as great as the Unseen One allows it to be."

"Get on with your trick, Draven," Mobeck said derisively from his chair.

"A trick? You'll see no tricks here—only miracles." He gazed at the crowd until many began to squirm in their seats. Then he noticed a guard with a machine gun standing next to the stage. "Are you a good shot with that?" he asked the guard.

"The best," the man said proudly.

"Good," Draven replied. "I want you to destroy the clock."

The guard looked puzzled. "What?"

"Take your machine gun and fire every bullet you have into the clock."

The guard turned to Mobeck, who was looking decidedly frustrated. "Do whatever he says," Mobeck ordered.

The guard pointed his weapon and fired away. At first the damage was hard to see, but then the face of the clock began to be chipped away, and shards of glass fell. Then the hands of the clock fell loose and limp, as if the clock itself had shrugged its shoulders and given up. When all was silent again, Draven turned to the crowd.

"What did that prove?" Mobeck challenged.

"Not only would it be a miracle for time to begin again," Draven answered, "but it would also be a miracle for that clock to run together with time. Yet, so they will."

He then held up his arms and closed his eyes. "O Lord of all, Holy One," he prayed aloud. "You have been mercifully patient with those who have turned their backs on You. Show us today that You, the Unseen One, are king over all and that I have done nothing except by Your power. Restore our lost time. Restore our lost hearts."

Draven stood where he was, his eyes closed and his arms raised. But nothing happened.

Mobeck sat up in his chair, now interested. "This is good," he said.

Draven didn't move.

The shattered clock was exactly the same as it was before. The crowd grew restless again. After an afternoon of nonsense, I figured they might riot now. I looked around uneasily. *Something has to happen*, I thought. The Unseen One wouldn't bring us to this point and let us down. *Please let something happen*, I found myself praying. *Please.*

Mobeck stood up. "This is very funny," he said, then called out to his guards, "Arrest this traitor!"

The guards moved toward Draven, who remained standing with his eyes closed and his arms held up.

"Look!" someone suddenly shouted. "The hand is moving!"

And it was. First the big hand shifted a little, then fell back, then moved again, slowly creeping up toward the number nine. Then the smaller hand came alive and moved past it, slowly reaching up and past the 12 and continuing around. The larger hand moved more quickly, as if it were in a race with the smaller hand. And then they both spun faster and faster until it seemed as if the entire clock tower started to shake. Suddenly, with an ear-shattering boom, it exploded into a million pieces.

The crowd began to scatter in an uproar. I turned, thinking they were afraid of the clock itself, but then I realized that other things were happening. The sky was ablaze with colors, flickering light and dark as if the sun were rising and setting, rushing to make up for three years of dormancy. I saw not one but *two* moons flying across the sky. Rain suddenly fell in great drops, followed by snow and sleet, thunder and lightning—all at once. People screamed and ran every which way. Many collapsed to the ground, clutching their heads or their stomachs and crying out in pain. A man who had been sitting behind me suddenly fell to the ground, and I could have sworn his hair went gray and wrinkles instantly appeared around his eyes and mouth. In rapid succession the trees grew leaves, which then changed colors, fell to the ground, and grew back again. Ivy crawled up the sides of the buildings, changing color and shape as it went. The grass grew under our feet. And meanwhile the sky continued to explode with light and dark.

Time was completely unleashed. The world was catching up the three years it had lost. Everyone and everything was thrown into convulsions of change. It was a terrifying and glorious thing to watch.

But, to my amazement, I didn't feel the effects of any of it.

I looked at Draven, who continued to pray. Mobeck, who'd fallen to his knees and was weeping with his face in his hands, was on the floor of the stage behind Draven.

When things seemed to start calming down, Draven leaned into the microphone and announced to whoever might still be listening, "These people who have led you astray will now pay the price for their apostasy."

I watched with horror as all the doctors, scientists, advisers, and even Skalaw's bizarre entourage suddenly twitched and flopped in their chairs as if they were being zapped with jolts of electricity. Their hair grew long and white, their skin went pale and wrinkled, and then, one by one, they fell over— dead from old age.

While this was happening, Mobeck sprang from the stage and ran to a car at the edge of the campus. He got in, and the car tore away.

"Draven," I shouted above the din, "Mobeck is getting away!"

Draven came down from the stage and gestured toward the horse-drawn wagons on the other end of the mall. "If we ride horses across the fields, we'll be able to catch up to him," he suggested.

"Horses?" I asked. "But I don't ride."

"Don't they teach kids *anything* in your world?" he groaned.

We made our way through the panicked crowd.

"We're going to get soaked," I said as a steady rain began to fall.

The owner of one of the horses seemed only too happy to let us use the animal, though whether he was truly happy or afraid, I couldn't tell. Draven climbed onto the horse's back.

"But where is Mobeck going?" I asked as Draven pulled me up behind him.

"Sarum will be in complete chaos. He'll try to hide in his private residence, near Deptford," he said. He nudged the horse with his heels, and we were off.

Across the newly green fields we galloped, out of one valley and into another. The rain slowed to a drizzle, but it felt like a full spray as we rode. Now that time had been restored, I could see how lush the country was. I was also dazzled by how much more brilliant the colors seemed than I'd ever seen in my own world. Off to my left, blue skies broke through the dark clouds and a full rainbow appeared.

"Maybe it's a sign," Draven shouted back to me.

Soon we reached a large plot of land with a low stone wall encircling orchards and vineyards. Draven tugged at the reins and said, "Whoa!" He guided the horse through a small break in the wall but didn't spur it back to speed.

"Why are we slowing down?" I asked.

"We're cutting through the private estate of Gwynn. Out of respect, I don't want to go too fast. Otherwise he might shoot us." Draven kept the horse at a steady pace.

"Why would he shoot us?"

"To protect himself. Mobeck and Skalaw have wanted this land for as long as Mobeck has been in power, and they sometimes send their goons over to try to 'persuade' Gwynn to sell. But he won't. It infuriates Mobeck and Skalaw."

"Why do they want the land so bad?"

"I think they want to build a swimming pool and some tennis courts on it," Draven replied, then spurred the horse to a quicker pace.

"Why don't Mobeck and Skalaw just take it away from him?"

"They wouldn't dare. Gwynn is too influential in Sarum."

Workers in a distant orchard stopped their work to look suspiciously at us. Draven waved in a friendly manner, but they didn't wave back. We reached another stone wall with a gate.

"This leads to Mobeck's private residence," Draven told me. "Let's walk from here."

After clearing the gate, Draven tied the horse to a tree, and we continued on foot. The rain had stopped completely now, but the water dripped from the branches over our heads.

Mobeck's private residence wasn't far beyond Gwynn's orchards. We came around the side of a sizable mansion made of red brick.

"No guards?" I asked.

Draven shrugged.

We circled around to the front of the mansion and stopped near the edge of the driveway leading to the front door. There was no sign of Mobeck's car.

"We may have gotten here before him," Draven said.

"What do we do, wait or knock?" I asked.

But the front door opened before Draven could answer. Lady Skalaw emerged from the house, stiff and erect. She was still dressed in the robes she'd worn at the university. Her face was red with rage.

"You dare to show your face here!" she snarled, her hands extended like claws.

I took a step back. My heart raced. I feared her more than anyone else.

Draven didn't betray any fear at all. He bowed formally, then said, "Lady Skalaw, your time is coming to an end."

"I should kill you this instant!"

"How? By dancing around me until I died of boredom?"

Skalaw stopped in her tracks as if she'd been slapped in the face. Suddenly she laughed. "You're full of yourself now, aren't you?" she said caustically. "Of course you would be. I watched your *magic* show on television. Most impressive."

"Not nearly as impressive as your own production," Draven taunted.

"Where is my husband?" she asked. "I assume he has joined your side, spineless fool that he is. The power went off to the television, so I didn't see the end of your spectacle. I have been waiting for him or my advisers to come and report."

"Your priests won't be coming," Draven told her. "But your husband should be here any minute."

"Where are my advisers?" she asked, the tension rising in her voice again.

Just then, Mobeck's car came down the drive toward us. It screeched to a halt, and Mobeck got out of the driver's seat. He looked wild-eyed and alarmed to see us there with Skalaw.

"What's going on here?" he asked breathlessly.

"I'm here to see that you finish what we began in Hailsham," Draven said. "You saw the undeniable display of the Unseen One's power. And unlike the other liars and false prophets, your lives He has spared."

"Where are my advisers?" Skalaw demanded again.

"They are dead," Mobeck replied.

Draven stepped forward. "Consider yourselves fortunate. The Unseen One has spared you to repent, to lead the nation back to Him."

"*Dead!*" Skalaw shrieked.

Mobeck stepped between Skalaw and Draven and pleaded, "Listen to me, Draven, these things take time. Go away for now and we'll talk about it another day."

"You killed my advisers?" Skalaw cried out.

"No excuses," Draven said to Mobeck. But I noticed that Draven was keeping an eye on Skalaw. To my surprise, Draven's face seemed to drain of color. Was he afraid?

Mobeck looked nervously at his wife, then back at Draven. "Please. Go for now," he begged. "This isn't a good time."

"Guards!" she screamed loudly as she picked up a stone from the driveway and threw it through one of the front windows. An alarm went off somewhere. "Guards! Guards! I want them seized!" She pointed to us, her long finger shaking with her fury. "I want them *killed!*"

"What do we do?" I asked Draven, backing away.

He was backing away, too. "I don't know," he stammered.

"You don't know?" I gasped. My legs went wobbly. If he didn't know, who did?

"It wasn't supposed to happen this way," he said.

I could hear voices inside the house. Men were coming.

"Kill them!" Skalaw screamed again and again.

"Draven?" I asked.

"Run," he said. "Run!"

We both dashed into the woods, retracing our path toward Gwynn's estate. Skalaw's voice seemed to penetrate the trees. A man's voice shouted instructions. The guards were giving chase. I heard the sound of a gun firing.

We ran like madmen and lost our direction. We soon came to Gwynn's wall, but we couldn't find the gate, so Draven gave me a leg up and hoisted me nearly the entire way over the wall. He pulled himself up and over and collapsed next to me.

"Where should we go?" I asked.

Draven rubbed his face. "I don't know," he said glumly. "Our horse is on the other side of the wall."

"Will Gwynn help us?"

"I don't know that either."

"What *do* you know?" I snapped, then regretted it. "I'm sorry."

Draven looked at me helplessly. "I thought they would repent," he said softly. "Restoring time was supposed to be the turning point. All was supposed to be well."

"The Unseen One told you that?"

"No. I assumed it." He lowered his head and said, "How could I have been so wrong?"

Skalaw's guards were on the other side of the wall now. "Should we climb over and get them?" one of them asked.

"You must be joking," came the second guard's reply. "Gwynn will shoot us on sight. Now that time has started again, bullets can do damage. For keeps."

"But we're on business for Supreme Commander Mobeck."

"It doesn't matter. We'll have to get some men together and go around to the front gate." With that, the guards left.

"Come on," Draven said. "We'll find a place to hide in the woods, just beyond the orchard."

We crossed a field and moved in among the trees. They looked like apple trees to me, the fruit hanging low and looking delicious. I suddenly felt hungry.

"Farther in," Draven beckoned.

The trees were planted in long rows, so we had to duck behind a tree, then run across a path to the next row, and so on. When we reached the end of the orchard, I could see the woods Draven had mentioned. They were about 100 yards away across an open field.

"Ready for a hard run?" Draven asked.

I wasn't, but I nodded that I was.

"Let's go."

We made a break for it. When we were about halfway across, however, my foot stepped into a rabbit hole. A sharp pain shot through my ankle, and I fell. "Draven!" I cried out.

Draven pulled me to my feet. "Can you walk?" he inquired.

I put some weight on my ankle, and it really hurt. "I think I sprained it or something," I reported.

"Grab onto me," he said as he put his arm around my waist.

We moved forward again but didn't get far. Off to our right, we heard the thunderous sound of horses' hooves on the ground. Riders were coming right at us.

"Faster!" Draven urged, pulling me toward the woods. But it was clear we wouldn't make it in time. The men on horseback were closing in.

Draven stopped. "Too late," he conceded. "It's no use."

We waited as the men pulled their horses up around us. I was relieved to see they weren't dressed in black-and-red uniforms but as ranch hands. My comfort was short-lived, though. Each man held a rifle.

"Trespassers!" a man with a beard shouted at us. "Come with us."

Chapter Ten

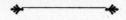

Gwynn was a large, broad-shouldered man with close-cropped, brown hair and a long mustache. His face was chiseled by years of outdoor work, his eyes narrow and his mouth firm. He wore a three-piece suit with a watch and fob in the vest pocket, which he occasionally fingered but never took out to read the time.

We were in Gwynn's house, in his study, which had dark wallpaper, a few shelves with various kinds of knickknacks, and a rolltop desk that was overrun with papers. He sat at the desk with his legs stretched out and his hands folded across his belly. We were sitting in two chairs across from him. The bearded ranch hand stood at the door, his rifle poised for action.

"I'm not a religious man," Gwynn said to Draven, "but I've always had a high regard for you. Your sense of justice is strong. Your refusal to kowtow to Mobeck or Skalaw is inspiring. I'm sure you know there is no love lost between those two and myself."

"I know," Draven replied.

In a voice full of scorn, Gwynn continued, "This land has been in my family for generations, and he wants me to sell it to him so he can build a swimming pool!"

"Mobeck is used to getting what he wants," Draven observed.

"So he is." Gwynn leveled his gaze at us. "But none of this explains what you're doing on my land."

"I assume you know what happened at the university," Draven began.

"I heard it on the radio, at least until the power went off. Then everything went crazy. I still haven't assessed the damage to my orchards. And I can't tell if I've lost livestock or gained some. We had birth and death all in a matter of minutes." Gwynn pointed to his temples. "This gray hair wasn't here this morning."

"The Unseen One has restored time—and killed the advisers to Mobeck and Skalaw," Draven explained.

"I wager they weren't very happy about that."

"Skalaw wants to kill me in revenge. We came onto your land to escape her guards."

Gwynn frowned. "And in so doing, you've put me in jeopardy for harboring you. Thank you very much."

We heard a knock at the door. The bearded man opened it, and someone whispered to him. He then turned to Gwynn and said, "We've got soldiers from Mobeck and Skalaw at the front door. They're searching for a couple of fugitives."

Gwynn looked at us thoughtfully. I waited, bracing myself to be handed over.

Gwynn instructed, "Tell the soldiers that I have guests and can't be bothered. They must take their search elsewhere. But," he added, "tell them I will be happy to report any fugitives I find once my guests have left."

The bearded man nodded and went out of the room.

"Thank you," Draven said.

"You may spend the night," Gwynn offered. "But I'll expect you to leave tomorrow. I don't want Mobeck to have any legitimate excuse to arrest me or to confiscate my lands."

"Would he dare?"

"In a heartbeat," Gwynn snorted.

Draven and I were shown to our rooms by a pretty woman who turned out to be Gwynn's wife, Karona. She spoke little but seemed eager to make sure we were comfortable. She apologized about my bedroom, which was closet-sized, though it held a bed, an end table, and a dresser. I told her it was very nice. She said she figured I'd be hungry after such a terrible ordeal and promised that dinner would be served soon.

I noticed that the shadows were moving slowly across the floor, so I went to the window and watched with fascination as the sun disappeared into the horizon. I imagined that most of the people around the world watched it now, moving as it hadn't moved for three years.

Karona served me my meal in my room. "Gwynn thinks it'll be better if the other members of the household and staff don't see you," she explained. "We may have spies among us."

"Thank you," I said gratefully.

She left while I ate. The food was good. It tasted like roast beef but was white like fish. I wondered if it was real or artificial.

Draven didn't join me, and I wondered what he was doing. After I finished eating, I crept into the hallway. I saw a tray full of untouched food next to his door and knocked softly.

"Draven?" I whispered, then knocked again. "Draven."

The door was unlocked from the other side and slowly opened. I put a hand to my mouth. Draven looked terrible. His hair was disheveled, as if he'd been tugging at it, and his eyes were red-rimmed from crying.

"Draven? What's wrong?"

Draven wiped his hand across his mouth. "Leave me alone," he said gruffly.

"No," I replied, taking a step into the room.

He put a hand on my shoulder to hold me back. "Don't come in. I'm busy."

"Doing what?"

"Praying," he said. "I can't be disturbed."

"You're upset about what happened with Skalaw."

He frowned at me. "You'd better believe I'm upset! And for that reason I need time alone with the Unseen One. He let me down, Scott. He brought me to this great moment and then hung me out to dry. I couldn't be more alone."

"You're not alone. I'm here," I reminded him.

A tiny smile crept across his lips. "You should go home now," he said and closed the door on me.

I knocked again. "But how?" I asked. "How am I supposed to go home?"

He didn't answer.

That night, the darkness covered us like a blanket. Owls that probably hadn't hooted for three years now exercised their vocal cords. Crickets chirped loudly. Somewhere in the distance, cows mooed and sheep bleated.

I lay in bed, worrying. What was wrong with Draven, and what was he going to do next? What did he mean by telling me to go home? Was I supposed to find my way back to that railway tunnel and hope it would lead me there?

I thought about my parents. In all the excitement, I hadn't thought about them much that day. I wondered if they missed me. Were they worried about me? Then I hoped that coming to Marus was the same as going to Narnia, where days, months, and years might pass while only seconds passed in your own world. If it worked that way, my parents wouldn't even know I was missing. They might never know.

I tried to picture their reactions when I told them about my adventure. My father would ask a lot of questions. He'd probably try to figure out the philosophy of it all. How could someone travel to a parallel world? Why would that world be so much like ours, and yet so different? Is there a way to travel back to it again? And then he would probably go to the railway tunnel and try to get into Marus himself.

My mother would listen to me and smile patiently, never betraying whether she believed me. If it really happened, she'd think it was because God wanted it to, and for a good purpose. If it were only something I made up, she'd think it was good that I had such a vivid imagination.

Both my parents always said I would do something special when I grew up. "You have the brains and the imagination to do wonderful things for God," Mom often said. "Your father and I keep waiting for the day when He'll tell you what He wants you to do." For that reason, I grew up believing that one day God would talk to me. I prayed and always expected some kind of answer. It's how I assumed things worked.

And right now, I wished God would say something. I wished He would tell me how to get home. But for the time being, I felt I should stick close to Draven.

I got up the next morning determined to help shake Draven out of his doldrums. Maybe he needed to rest somewhere away from all the trouble. *We could escape somewhere,* I thought. *Maybe he could come to my world with me for a while.*

I slipped out of my room and went to Draven's door just as Gwynn came down the hall. "He's not there," Gwynn said.

"What?" I asked, my mouth going dry and the blood draining out of my face. "Where is he?"

Gwynn held up a piece of paper. "This was on the kitchen table when we woke up this morning. It's a note from Draven."

He handed me the paper.

In clear handwriting, it said:

> Gwynn,
>
> Thank you for the hospitality and protection. I have gone to Eastcliff to pray and meditate. Take care of the boy. He'll be no trouble to you.
>
> *Draven*

I stared at the note, dumbfounded. "He left me?" I asked, not believing it.

"I'm afraid so."

"But how could he?" My eyes burned. This was wrong. It was a terrible mistake.

"It's probably for the best," Gwynn said in a matter-of-fact tone. "Mobeck and Skalaw want to kill Draven, not you. By leaving, he's put you out of danger."

"But what am I going to do?" I asked. "Where should I go?"

"He didn't say. But you're welcome to stay here for a while."

I leaned against the wall, my head swimming. Now I couldn't go home *or* follow Draven. I shoved the note into my pocket and rubbed my face.

That day crawled by at a snail's pace. I lingered around the house like a bored child, getting in people's way and feeling sorry for myself. Karona offered to play games with me, but that made me feel like a baby, so I said no, thanks. Gwynn got tired of my moping and decided it was worth the risk to send me out to the orchard to collect apples with his workers. It was soon obvious that he had told the foreman of the crew to work me hard. He did, in spite of my sprained ankle. I was so busy that I didn't have time to think about how unfortunate I was.

I did the same thing the next day and the day after that. The days went by quickly, and I was so tired that I slept soundly at night. I also started to get the feeling that everything was going to be all right somehow. God—the Unseen One—was going to take care of me.

One night at supper, Gwynn announced that he was going to Hailsham for a city council meeting. "Something is going on," I heard him tell Karona. "I got a message from three of the members telling me not to miss it. I have a feeling Mobeck and Skalaw might be trying to get our land again."

"You can't trust them," Karona reminded him anxiously. "How will I know you're all right?"

Gwynn pondered the question for a while, trying to decide how to get word back to Karona if something went wrong at the meeting. "All our servants and workers are known to Mobeck's police," he finally began. "If he tries anything treacherous with me, he's sure to have them arrested."

"What if you take somebody the police don't know?" I asked. "Like who?"

"Me," I said. "They don't know me. I could sneak in, and if anything happens, I could run home and warn Karona."

At first Gwynn said no. But the more he thought about it, the better the idea seemed. Finally he agreed to take me with him.

I was grateful. Not only did I want to get out of the house for a while, but I also wanted to feel like I was helping him. The plan was for me to call Karona from the public phone at the city hall.

As we drove to Hailsham in his car, Gwynn gave me a map with the directions home clearly marked. "If anything does happen—and probably nothing will—run back to the house as fast as you can after you've made the call. It's three miles by car, but you can make it quicker cutting across country."

"Draven and I did the same thing," I told him. "The day when time restarted, we got to Mobeck's house before he did."

The city hall was just off Hailsham's main street. I waited in the car while Gwynn went in. Dozens of people also made their way up the steps and disappeared inside. Then, when the stream of traffic died down and I didn't think anyone was paying attention, I got out of the car and headed in. I looked for any sign of Mobeck, Skalaw, or their guards but didn't see them. It was evening now, and the building seemed dark and empty. I could hear voices coming from a room and saw light spilling out onto the floor at the end of the center hall.

I crept to the door and slipped into the back of a large meeting room. The council members sat at a table at the far end. The room was full of people in chairs set up to accommodate an audience. A man at the center of the table was droning on about the damage done to the water system because of Draven's "evil trickery." Another man complained about the difficulties of maintaining electricity because of what Draven had done. A woman then grumbled about the new strain on the other health and public services.

I couldn't believe what I was hearing. The Unseen One had restored time and allowed life to return to its natural state, and these politicians were griping about it!

Gwynn looked bored. At one point he glanced up at me, rolled his eyes, and looked away again.

Finally the chairman at the center—at least, I assumed he was the chairman—asked if anyone present had other items to bring to the council's attention.

Suddenly one of the audience members stood up. "I have

a grievance against Gwynn," the man said in a thick voice. It was Tesdor!

Gwynn sat up straight.

"What's your grievance?" the chairman asked.

"I have evidence that Gwynn has been in cahoots with an enemy of the state."

"Nonsense!" Gwynn said.

Tesdor held up a large folder. "I have photos in here of Gwynn conspiring with Draven himself no less than *three hours* after Draven's plot against our supreme commander and his wife failed."

His plot failed? I wondered, open-mouthed. *But time was restored!* I wanted to shout.

Gwynn seemed unconcerned. "Go back and tell your bosses it won't work," he said to Tesdor. "Everyone here knows that the supreme commander and Lady Skalaw will do anything to get my land. But this council is wise to their ways and won't fall for your tricks."

Another man I hadn't seen before stood up. "Is that so?" he challenged. "Then the council is willing to ignore photos *and* testimony that will prove you are a coconspirator with Draven?"

"Show your photos!" Gwynn dared him. "Bring out your testimony!"

A projector was brought in, a screen set up, and the lights dimmed. Blurred photos were splashed onto the screen of Gwynn talking to someone. It might have been Draven, or it might have been someone else. The photos weren't clear enough to prove either case.

"That might easily be one of my workers," Gwynn said.

"Ah," replied the mystery man, "but our testimony will confirm that it was Draven himself."

"Testimony from whom?" Gwynn asked.

The lights came up again and a thin, weaselly-looking man stood up, his hat in his hand. "I saw you talking to Draven," the man declared in a high voice.

Gwynn looked closely at the man. "Who are you?" he demanded.

"I'm a man in your employ."

Gwynn looked closer, then smiled. "You're a man who *was* in my employ. I fired you last week for trying to steal from me. You couldn't have seen me talking to Draven—or *anyone*—this week."

"But I saw you!" the man shouted, his voice squeaking. "You and Draven are old friends!"

Gwynn leaned back in his chair. "This is ridiculous," he growled. "I beg the council to clear the room of these hacks."

The council members all looked away from Gwynn, their eyes fixed on other things. No one moved. The chairman didn't say anything.

"Well?" Gwynn asked. "Can we get on with our meeting or not?"

Still no one spoke.

"Then *I'll* do it." Gwynn pointed at his accusers. "As a fully endowed member of this council, I demand that you leave this meeting immediately. We won't tolerate thieves and liars, no matter who they work for!"

"Liars!" Tesdor exclaimed as he leaped to his feet. His chair fell back with a crash.

It was clear to me later that this was a cue. As soon as Tesdor got up, people began to shout and shove each other. More chairs were knocked over, and it looked as if a riot had started, but there was something fake about it. For all the pushing and yelling, no one seemed to get hurt.

Someone brushed past me then, almost knocking me over. It was a man in a black-and-red uniform. Then came another and another. The first man blew a shrill whistle and shouted, "Break it up! You're under arrest!"

More confusion followed as the council members and people in the audience shouted their protests. Then, in the thick of it, fingers were pointed at Gwynn as if *he'd* started the trouble. Tesdor and his cronies reiterated their claim that Gwynn was a traitor who had helped Draven. They waved their blurred photos and got the thin man to say again what he'd supposedly seen.

That seemed like enough evidence for the head of the police, who now threw in the charge that Gwynn had come to the meeting to incite a riot. Two officers grabbed Gwynn and started to drag him out. The council members again stayed in their seats without saying a word in Gwynn's defense.

"This is a setup!" Gwynn cried out. Then he shouted at the council members, "How much did they pay you?"

I tried to get out before the rest of the crowd and rushed down the hallway to the front door and the nearby public phone box. More police were milling around, waiting, and a crowd gathered. I heard a commotion back down the hall. I turned in time to see that a scuffle had broken out in the crowd surrounding Gwynn. It was too dark to see who was doing what. Then a shot rang out. A woman screamed.

One of the policemen charged up the stairs and knocked me aside. "What happened?" he called out.

"Gwynn's been shot!" someone answered. "He was trying to escape!"

I felt sick in my stomach and knew what had really happened.

"Stop that boy!" Tesdor shouted from behind me.

I bolted for the door. There was no chance to make a call now. I had to get to Karona to warn her. I ran outside to the porch and, as I descended the steps, yelled at the policemen, "Someone's been shot! The assassin is trying to escape!"

The police ran up the stairs, just in time to collide with Tesdor and his men as they came out the door. I sprinted down an alley that led to a field behind the village. This was the way back, I knew.

I ran as fast as I could across the dark fields, following the paths Gwynn had told me about. Only once did I have to stop to look at the map, using the light of the two full moons to see.

As I got closer to Gwynn's estate, I saw a strange orange and red glow in the sky. I thought it was some other freak of nature—another miracle of Draven's—until I realized what it was. Gwynn's house was on fire. I reached the front gate and found two policemen posted there.

"You can't go in there," one of them told me.

"What happened?" I asked, a sick feeling rising in my throat.

"A terrible accident. No survivors," he replied. "Now go home."

I heard sirens coming—or it might have been a high-pitched scream of panic in my brain. I turned and let the tears fall as I ran into the darkness.

CHAPTER ELEVEN

Since I didn't know where to go after getting clear of Gwynn's property, I walked aimlessly for what seemed like miles and miles. Eventually, I found a barn in the middle of a field. It was covered and had plenty of hay in it, so I hid myself and prayed that the Unseen One would help me figure out what to do in the morning. I fell asleep.

I had a vivid dream about my parents. They were sitting by a fire in a cave. My father was in his favorite easy chair, reading a book. My mother was doing the crossword puzzle in the newspaper. Then suddenly my mother looked up at me and said, "We always knew you would do something special for God. He gave you to us when we thought we'd never have a child. But we must give you back to Him. Go to Eastcliff."

"But I don't know where it is," I complained.

My father looked over his glasses at me impatiently. "Use your head, son," he instructed.

Voices woke me the next morning. I sat up, then scrambled farther into the hay to keep from getting in trouble.

"You don't have to hide," a woman said. "We've already seen you. We were going to let you sleep longer." I peeked out of the stack of hay. A pleasant-looking, heavyset woman was leaning down toward me, wiggling a finger. "Come on out."

I crawled out into full view. The woman was there with a man, who was also pleasant-looking and heavyset.

"Thank you," I said as I dusted myself off. "I was lost and tired and—"

"You don't have to explain," the man said. "In these difficult days, we often find people in our barn."

The woman nodded. "Yes, we've become an unofficial crossing point on the border. Fugitives, politicians, refugees—they all come through here."

"Border?" I asked, puzzled. "What border?"

"The border between East and West Marus," the woman said.

I was crestfallen. "You mean I walked to the other country without meaning to?"

The man shoved a pitchfork into the hay, as if to remove any hint that I'd been in it. "Whether you meant to or not, you did. You are now in East Marus."

"Aren't you happy to be away from that wicked tyrant and his wife?" the woman asked.

"I'm happy to be away from them, I guess. But not if it's put me farther away from Eastcliff."

"Farther away?" The man looked at the woman, and they both laughed. "Where do you think Eastcliff is?"

"I don't know," I admitted.

"Use your head," the woman playfully scolded me. "Where do you think *East*cliff might be?"

"In East Marus?" I guessed.

They both applauded my intelligence. Then the woman said, "Come inside. We can give you a nice breakfast now that the chickens are laying eggs again. Then we'll show you where Eastcliff is."

The man's name was Londor, and the woman's name was Idyll. As best as I could make out from their conversation, they were a "stop" on a sort of Underground Railroad from West to East Marus. People who needed to escape Mobeck and Skalaw came through this part of the country since it didn't have many proper roads and wasn't as heavily guarded. And only when

Londor pulled out a map of Marus did I see that Hailsham was just a few miles from the East Marus border. I had stumbled onto it by accident—or with the help of the Unseen One.

To my surprise, Marus was all shoreline on the east, where it met the Alconian Sea. Eastcliff was a small village on the northern shore. I was disheartened to learn that it would take several days of hard walking to get there. It occurred to me, too, that Draven might not be there when I arrived.

I looked at the map again and saw that Raundale was in the northern territory of West Marus. Maybe if I went there, I could find the railway tunnel and go back to my own world again? Maybe. But it was also possible that the railway tunnel was one-way into Marus and not a way out. Only the Unseen One, or maybe Draven, could get me home.

So with a full stomach, a packed lunch, and a heavy heart, I left Londor and Idyll. I headed north on Albany Road and wished I had my driver's license or, at the very least, a bike.

After a few miles, I came to a sign indicating that a railway station was nearby. If I went just north of the station, I reasoned, I might be able to catch a train as it left the station, before it picked up speed, and jump into an open car as I had done with Draven.

The idea seemed like a good one, and the station wasn't much more than a shack with a ticket office. I followed the tracks a little way up from the station and waited behind a tree.

After about an hour, a train pulled in from the south, let its passengers off, then came my way. I tried to gauge its speed and raced alongside, hoping it had an open car. One came by. I ran harder and was barely able to grab onto a ladder bolted to the side. Remembering to keep my legs clear of the wheels and tracks, I pulled up with all my might, swinging myself into the car. I collapsed onto the floor to catch my breath.

"And what do we have here?" a voice said.

I looked up. A toothless old man with scuzzy, white whiskers leaned over me.

"Hi," I said with a gasp.

"Hi yourself. Have you got fare for my car?" the old man asked.

I sat up. The car was empty except for the dirt and straw on its floor. We were alone. "Fare?" I asked.

"You'd better have something for me or I'll throw you off."

I glanced out the open door. The train was picking up speed. To jump off now would do me a lot of damage. "What kind of fare?" I inquired.

The old man looked at my packed lunch. "What's in there?" he asked.

"Lunch."

He snatched the bag away from me with a speed I wouldn't have thought possible. "That'll do." He retreated to the rear of the car and tore into my bag.

I sat at the other end of the car and watched him eat my lunch. I tried to be friendly and asked him questions, but he talked like a broken record about a garden he once had and how many potatoes he grew on it. "Half a ton!" he said.

Apart from that, we sat in silence.

The journey was long, hard on my rear end, and boring. I didn't dare go to sleep for fear that the old man might try to steal something else from me, like my shoes. We stopped at various stations along the way, but no one bothered with our car. It started to rain, and the old man moved to my end of the car because the rain was blowing back onto him. He jabbered again about the garden he once had and how many potatoes he grew on it. "A ton!" he boasted.

It was getting late in the afternoon, and I started to feel my hunger. The old man's talk of potatoes didn't help.

As night approached, I started to wonder how far north we'd gone. I didn't want to go too far or I'd miss Eastcliff and have to double back. I thought about asking the old man but wasn't confident he'd give me the right answer. I decided to take a chance and get off before we reached the next station.

An hour later, the train started to slow down. Peeking out the door, I saw a large city up ahead. When it seemed safe, I said good-bye to the old man, who had fallen asleep, and jumped off. I then walked along the tracks up to the station itself.

In the station I found a wall map. I was in a town called Fangettal. With relief, I saw that I was due west of Eastcliff. On the map, it didn't look like a very long walk at all.

Not far from the station, I found an abandoned shack. It might have been used by railway workers at one time, but it looked as if it could shelter me from the rain. It would do until morning. I curled up for a good night's sleep.

The rain continued all night and started to leak through the roof. No matter where I moved in the shed, I either got hit by the slow drips or splashed by them after they hit the floor. At dawn, the rain stopped and I gave up trying to sleep anymore. I came out of the shed and was stopped cold by a shock. To the east, the direction I had to go, lay a vast, open country— and mountains. They were large, rounded mountains, the kind that stand out like the shoulders on a hunched-over man.

"Oh, no!" I moaned. Eastcliff was somewhere on the other side of those mountains. With a deep groan, I started the difficult journey.

At first the going was easy. I walked across green meadows and through groves of trees. I took a chance and ate some wild berries from a patch of bushes. They tasted good and didn't seem to hurt me. I stopped by a gurgling stream and drank the freshest water I'd ever had. Then the incline began and the hills grew bigger. Their sides were splashed with the yellows, reds, and purples of wildflowers. Soon thereafter, I headed into a thick forest. My breathing became heavier as no clear path presented itself. I made my way over fallen trees, around thick patches of bushes, and through damp leaves. I could smell the wet and the wood all around. Birds teased me. Somewhere in the distance, I heard a growl. Did they have bears in this country? I didn't know and certainly didn't want to think about it.

I came upon another stream that seemed to cut through the forest and up into the mountain and decided to follow it. If worse came to worst, I wouldn't be thirsty, I figured.

The stream meandered up the mountainside and, hours later, got me near the top before it seemed to disappear into a thicket. I went on without it, and when I thought I was at the very top, I turned, hoping for a view of where I'd been. Unfortunately, the trees were too high and the woods were too thick. The same was true for the direction in which I was headed. Every muscle in my body ached now. I considered stopping for a while but concluded it would be a waste of daylight. I pressed onward down the other side of the mountain.

More than once, I wondered where all this was going to lead me. I might find Draven in Eastcliff, but he might not want to see me. He had deserted me, after all. And it was possible that he didn't know how to get me home again. Then where would I be?

I had more berries for dinner and wished I had been a Boy Scout or something useful. I was probably surrounded by wonderfully edible things and didn't know it.

It started to get dark, and I thought about where I would sleep. After searching for a while, I found a large wreck of a tree that had fallen over in such a way as to provide shelter beneath it. I collected loose branches and made a tent around the section of the tree where I hoped to sleep. The ground underneath was only slightly damp. I prayed that the Unseen One would protect me from bears, snakes, and anything else that might mistake me for a meal. For a long time, every sound from the woods—and the growling of my own nearly-empty stomach—kept me awake. I dozed.

Tired and stiff, I got up the next morning and felt a bad mood fall over me like a cloudburst. I trudged down the mountain, grumbling the whole way. *What if I reach the bottom and there's another mountain to go over? And another after that? What if there are a dozen mountains to cross to get to Eastcliff? What if Draven isn't there? Why can't the Unseen One make this easier for me? After all, it wasn't my idea to come to Marus. I didn't ask to witness everything that had happened.*

As if to confirm my darkest worries, the woods thinned out and I came to a clearing that gave me a view of what lay ahead. Another mountain stood before me, this one even higher than the one I'd just crossed. I slumped down where I was, exhausted and discouraged, and felt like having a good cry. And I might have, but then I saw a ribbon of black cutting up into the mountain. I followed it down to the valley below with my eye and realized that it crossed somewhere directly in front of me.

A road!

And if there was a road, there might be a car or a truck driven by someone who'd give me a ride.

Hopeful, I got up and walked on with a purposeful spring in my step. Two hours later, I reached the road. It was old and pot-holed. Did anyone ever use it? I looked in both directions. No one was in sight. Should I follow it in the hopes that someone might come along, or was it smarter to carry on straight up the mountain?

Help me, I asked the Unseen One. *Which is the best way to go?*

The answer came in a tiny sliver of smoke that drifted from amidst the trees, just around a bend in the road toward the north. "Where there's smoke, there's fire," I muttered to myself and headed in that direction.

The distance was deceptive. It took half an hour to get to the bend. The smoke came from the chimney of a small cottage. Next to it was an old-fashioned diner called the One-Stop Café. I had no money for food, but I thought I could at least ask how far it was to Eastcliff. I tried the door handle, but it was locked. A sign handwritten in a terrible scrawl said, "Ring the bell," so I did.

"Coming, coming!" a man shouted from the cottage and came hustling over to me, tying an apron around his waist. When he realized I was only a kid, he slowed down. "It's the slack time of year," he said. "I only open the café if someone comes."

"I don't have any money for food," I explained.

He stopped where he was. He was a middle-aged man with short, black hair and a wiry mustache. "I'm not a charity," he said gruffly.

"I just wanted to ask how far it is to Eastcliff."

"Once you get over the mountain, it's about 30 miles. Maybe 40. Might be 50, come to think of it."

"Oh," I said. "Thanks."

The man looked as if he might turn around and go back to the cottage, but he couldn't resist asking, "What are you doing way out here? We don't get many people unless they're in some kind of car or truck. Did you walk?"

I nodded. "Yes, sir."

"Are you a runaway?"

"No, sir. I was left behind by accident, and now I'm going to Eastcliff to meet someone."

The man cocked an eyebrow. "Left behind *where* by accident?"

"Hailsham or Deptford—I'm not sure."

"They're close to each other. And you've come all this way? Well, that sounds even stranger. Good luck." He now turned to go.

"Sir," I began, not sure of what I wanted to say. "I was wondering if there was any chance of working for some food. I don't need much. Just a sandwich or something."

The man considered the idea. "Okay. I'd like to get some wood chopped before winter. Come inside and eat. Then I'll show you what I need done."

We went into the diner. It was all chrome, with a long counter and red-topped stools on one side and booths on the other. The man went behind the counter to the grill. He pointed to a bright-red menu and asked, "What are you hungry for? We've got a full menu again, what with the resumption of time."

Everything on the menu made me so hungry that my stomach ached. I chose a lunch special that included something that looked like an oversized hamburger, cut potatoes (like french fries), and a drink.

The man threw the burger on the grill and turned on a small black-and-white television while he cooked it. The sound was down, but the news report showed clips from what had happened at the University of Hailsham. I saw Mobeck and his various advisers, Skalaw and her dancing priests, and, of course, Draven. The film showed him with his eyes closed and hands held in the air, and then the camera cut to the large clock as the hands spun wildly. The picture suddenly broke up.

"Boy, that was something," the man said, waving a spatula at the television.

"I know," I said. "I was there."

The man spun on his heel to face me. "You're pulling my leg."

"No, sir. I was in the front row when it happened."

He eyed me carefully. "I don't take well to liars."

"I'm not lying! I was there with Draven, and then we—"

"You were *with* Draven?" the man asked, dumbfounded.

"That's who I'm supposed to meet in Eastcliff."

The man still looked at me with a mixture of suspicion and awe. He obviously didn't know whether to believe me. "Prove it," he finally said.

I tried to think of a way but didn't know how.

"Prove it and you'll get your meal for free," he continued. "I'll even throw in dinner. In fact, you can stay in my guest room." He leaned on his elbows and tipped his head my way, as if telling me a secret. "I'm a believer, you know. In the Unseen One."

I shook my head. "I don't know how to prove it to you. I was there with him, I saw everything that happened, but I don't have anything to prove it."

"That's too bad," the man said. Then he thought of something. "I have a picture of Draven. He even autographed it for me a few years ago, right before time stopped."

The man reached under the counter and pulled out a framed photo of Draven. It was the same photo I'd seen in the magazine. *It doesn't look much like him now,* I thought. At the bottom, in Draven's handwriting, it said, "Keep the faith. Draven."

"Wait a minute," I said and slid off the stool. "I have proof!" I rifled through my pockets and pulled out the note

Draven had written back at Gwynn's house. I handed it to the man. "Draven wrote this. I'm the boy he referred to. You can compare the handwriting if you want proof."

The man looked at the note and then the photo. He clucked his tongue thoughtfully. "Well, there you are," he said happily. Holding out his hand to me, he said, "I'm Byngriff."

I shook his hand. "My name is Scott."

The smell of the hamburger on the grill filled the diner. Things were looking up.

CHAPTER TWELVE

❖——————❖

"I can take you as far as the downs," Byngriff said over breakfast the next morning.

"What are the downs?" I asked.

Byngriff looked at me, surprised. "The *downs.*"

I shrugged.

"Downs are—" He stopped himself and frowned. "Oh, everyone knows what the downs are."

"I don't."

"The downs are ... they're the open countryside, the rolling, green land. Sometimes they have trees. They're mostly used as pasture. Do you understand?"

"I think I do," I replied. I figured I would recognize them when I saw them.

"Eat up. We have to go," he said.

Since Byngriff had realized that I was somehow connected to Draven, he had treated me like royalty. I had eaten a hearty lunch and a full dinner and slept in a warm, dry bed. Byngriff had insisted it was all a pleasure for him, but I insisted on chopping some wood to help pay him back. He reluctantly let me do it, but I noticed he gave me the smallest logs to do.

"Once we get over the next mountain and head toward the sea, we'll come to the downs," Byngriff explained. "You can't miss them. Eastcliff is on the other end. I'd drive you all the way, but it's a windy road and I can't be away from my diner that long. People tend to break in and help themselves to my food when I'm not here."

"I don't want to take you out of your way," I said. But I

was secretly grateful not to have to go over the mountain on foot.

"My pleasure. And who knows? Maybe we'll bump into Draven along the way and I can say hello again."

I hoped Byngriff's wish would come true.

The road over the mountain and down the other side was full of tortuous curves. The crossing took nearly two hours in Byngriff's old pickup truck. At one point along the way, I had a view of the scene below. I could see how the downs spilled one hill over another, like rippling, green waves, toward the blue sea beyond.

At the bottom of the mountain, Byngriff pulled off the road and let me out. "Thank you for everything," I said warmly, shaking his hand.

He smiled, then pointed to the east. The view was exactly as he had described: open and rolling fields of green. "Straight across those downs is where you'll find Eastcliff," he said. "I hope the Unseen One will guide you."

"Me, too."

I closed the door and stepped away as he circled the truck around and headed back for his home. With a false sense of confidence, I made my way into the downs. *I'm nearly there,* I thought. *It should be easy now.*

But it wasn't. Halfway across the downs, which were bigger than they had looked from a distance, it began to rain. I eventually reached a small village that bore the name of Eastcliff. It had an inn, a combination post office and grocery store, and a handful of cottages scattered off a single dirt road. The woman at the post office said that she'd seen Draven several days before, but not since. When I asked if he might be staying at the inn, she replied, "I doubt it. He never does when he comes here."

"Does he stay in one of the cottages?" I suggested.

"Not that I know of." She scratched at her chin. "Come to think of it, I don't know where he stays when he comes here. I don't think anybody knows. We reckoned it was none of our business."

"Then how am I supposed to find him?"

The woman squinted as if looking for an idea. "I guess you'll have to go house to house. If he's still in the area, someone's bound to have seen him. Other than that, you'll have to hike up and down the coast. Maybe you'll happen upon him that way."

I looked out at the falling rain. Neither idea seemed good to me, but I didn't have a choice.

From cottage to cottage I went, asking the same question: "Have you seen Draven?" Most of the people I met were friendly—a couple of them even gave me brief shelter from the rain, cups of tea, and cookies—but they didn't know where Draven was. Others were more suspicious and gave me the impression that even if they'd seen him, they wouldn't tell me.

Finally, after the rain had stopped late in the afternoon, I met an old man walking a dog. He was obviously hard of hearing and shouted in response to my question, "Ravens? No, not around this time of year!"

"*Draven*," I corrected him. "A tall man, looks like a movie star."

"A moving *what?*"

I groaned and spoke loudly and slowly. "He's a *voice* for the *Unseen One.*"

The man looked at me as if he were trying to work out in his mind what I'd just said. Then he nodded briskly and shouted, "Oh, yes, Draven! I see him from time to time, walking on the beach! Doesn't talk much! Just a nod and a hello!"

"When did you last see him?" I asked hopefully.

"It might have been yesterday! Or last week!" He tipped up his cap and scratched his head. "Or am I confusing that with last year? You know, I got awfully confused when the sun got stuck!"

"Do you know where he lives when he comes here?"

"Don't be ridiculous!" the old man yelled with a frown. "He doesn't give me anything! We say hello, that's all!"

"*Lives,*" I said louder. "Do you know where he *lives.*"

"Never noticed!" the old man replied. "Good day!" He whistled for his dog, who'd wandered off to more-interesting places, and strolled away.

So my only clue was that Draven sometimes walked along the beach. I shrugged to no one and ventured that way, trekking straight across the wind-swept downs to the sea beyond. Before long, I discovered what no one had told me— namely, that the downs came to a very *high* dead end at the shore. A sheer, white cliff dropped down to the beach and the water hundreds of feet below. Just offshore was a red-and-white-striped lighthouse. I was amazed. I never thought I'd be in a position to look *down* on a lighthouse.

"I guess this is why they call it East*cliff*," I said to myself.

I paced up and down the edge, peering over where I could, in hopes of seeing a way down. I couldn't find anything. I looked to the north and then the south. Miles away, in either direction, it looked as if the land sloped to meet the sea. But I didn't want to walk that far just to walk all the way back again. There had to be a way down.

I slowly walked north, watching the edge for any sign of a break or a path. I had several false alarms and nearly slipped over the side once but found nothing. Finally, just as the sun began to sink, I saw what looked like a grassy path angling downward. I went up to it carefully, testing my footing along the way, and peered over. The path seemed to lead down to a ragged cliff. From there, it looked as though the rocky terrain sloped more gently to the beach. *This must be the way*, I thought and stepped more bravely.

After going only a few dozen feet down the path, I realized the ragged cliff was higher above the rocky terrain than I'd thought. A gap of 30 or 40 feet existed between the cliff and the start of the rocks below. I'd never be able to bridge that without a rope, I knew. Discouraged, I turned to go back up to the top.

The return should have been easy. But it had started to rain again, making the grass slick. I found myself slipping a lot. My heart pounded one time as I slid near the very edge, catching sight of the waves and rocks far below before I skidded to a stop. I got on all fours and started again.

Near the top of the path, I sighed with relief and stood up straight—and instantly lost my footing again. I screamed as I slid downward, coming close to the edge of the path. Down and down I went until, with a bump against a large rock, I stopped at the lower cliff's border. A seagull gave me an indignant look, shook its feathers, and took off. I slowly stood up. My back and legs hurt, but I was all right.

The rain fell more heavily now. I looked at the path and knew I'd never get back up while it was so wet. But I didn't much like the idea of being stuck on this cliff, either. I glanced around. The beach, waves, and rocks were still a long way down. Then something caught my eye, and I quickly turned around. There was a cave in the cliff face.

If I'd thought about it, I might have been too afraid to go straight in. But the rain was pouring down, and I was already soaked to the skin, so in I went. The cave was dry at least. I felt around in the dark, praying that I wouldn't put my hand in anything disgusting. My fingers brushed against something furry, and I dashed out onto the path again. I watched the cave, expecting a bear or something equally horrible to come out after me. It didn't. Not a sound or a movement came from within.

I couldn't stay in the rain, I knew, so I ventured back into the cave, thoughts of something hairy and dead filling my head. I reached out again to the fur. Whatever it had been in life, it was dead enough now—dead and skinned, in fact. My elbow bumped something that felt like a wooden crate. I heard a rattle of glass and metal. I felt around on the top of the crate and found matches. I hoped they were dry enough to light. After one or two false sparks, a flame came to life, giving me a dim view of my surroundings.

The first thing I saw was an oil lamp. That was the rattle of glass and metal I'd heard. There was oil left in the base. I took off the glass top and lit the wick. It spat at me and then slowly burned blue, then yellow and red.

The cave had been a home to someone. Several large furs lay on the floor. I assumed it was a makeshift bed. To my eye, it looked comfortable enough to sleep in. Empty cardboard boxes were scattered around. Even a pair of old-fashioned eyeglasses sat nearby.

A pirate's den, I thought and imagined buried treasure somewhere deep in the cave. But it wasn't that deep—only a dozen feet beyond where I now sat. Whoever had furnished this cave had also piled some dead brush to the side. I could see the black stain where a fire had been made. I followed suit. Using the cardboard boxes as kindling, I got a fire going. The natural draft of the cave sent the smoke outside.

"Thank You," I said aloud to the Unseen One as the heat dried my wet clothes.

Night came, the rain stopped, and the clouds cleared the way for Marus's two moons to come out. They reflected brightly on the water, and for a while I felt cozy and contented. I went to the edge of the cliff and looked over. I never would have survived that fall. *Something else to be thankful for,* I thought.

A yellow glow farther up the beach caught my eye. It was a fire. Someone was down there, moving back and forth in front of the flames. I got the impression he was pacing. Could it be Draven? I cupped my hands around my mouth and shouted at the top of my lungs, "Draven!"

The pacing continued. Whoever it was probably couldn't hear me because of the waves. I shouted a couple more times, but nothing happened. I kept watching. What was he doing down there? He paced for another minute, and then it looked as though he sat down by the fire. Or was he kneeling? I squinted, trying to see more clearly. He was definitely kneeling, and his arms were raised to the sky. It reminded me of how he had looked when time was restored.

Then a strange thing happened. Out of the clear night sky, another storm came. Thunder rolled, lightning flashed, and rain blew in on a gale—all without clouds. I retreated into the cave and watched it all, bewildered. The two moons were still there in a clear sky, but the storm raged on.

"What in the world is going on here?" I asked out loud.

Then, just as suddenly as it had come, the storm stopped. I crept out onto the cliff again and looked down at the man on the beach. The fire still blazed, and he stayed on his knees with his arms held up.

Am I dreaming? I wondered. Surely a storm like that would have put out the fire and driven the man to safety. But there he remained, as if nothing had happened.

I watched him for another moment. He didn't move from his position. The night seemed quiet and calm. Then, out of the corner of my eye, I saw something move on the sea. I thought it might have been a large ship or maybe even a giant sea creature, but it wasn't. The sea itself seemed to rise up, slowly at first, like a hill growing on the horizon. Higher and higher it went until the two moons were blocked from my view.

Though I'd never seen one before, I knew what it was. "A tidal wave," I gasped, and it was headed straight for us!

"Draven!" I shouted again and again. But the man below didn't move. He didn't seem to notice what was coming at him from the sea.

The water climbed even higher, and I backed away into the cave. My mouth went dry and my legs felt spindly. Could that wave reach as high as my cave? If it could, there was no hope for either of us. I went as far back into the cave as I could, and pressed against the cold, stone wall. I watched the wave come, roaring now like a ferocious grizzly, getting bigger and bigger until it was all I could see from the mouth of the cave.

"Help me!" I whispered to the Unseen One.

The enormous wave came down with a wild, churning, bubbling fury.

Chapter Thirteen

I pushed and kicked against the wave with all my might. The furs that had covered me were thrown aside.

The flickering light from my fire bounced on the walls. All was quiet. All was dry. The two moons hung higher than they had been before. There was no sign of a storm or a wave.

"A dream?" I gasped, still feeling the effects of it on my nerves. "It was a dream?"

I climbed to my feet and went out to the cliff. It wasn't entirely a dream, I thought. The fire still burned on the beach, and the kneeling man still held his hands up in the air. I slumped onto the ground. "Unless *this* is a dream, too," I said. I thought about it for a moment. *Could I be having a dream— or a dream within a dream—when I think I'm wide awake?*

I pinched myself. "Ouch," I whispered and rubbed the small, red welt I'd made.

"What's going on here?" I asked out loud, looking up. The Unseen One could hear me without my speaking out loud, but it felt better to hear my own voice. "Please tell me what this means."

I looked down at the man on the beach. He was no longer holding his hands up but had fallen facedown into the sand. I had no doubt it was Draven. And then I had a sudden and reassuring feeling that whatever had happened wasn't really for me at all. It had happened for *him*. Like all the other supernatural things I'd seen, I had seen them as they'd happened to Draven.

So once again I was his witness. That's what he had called me back at the start, a witness.

"Is that why I'm here?" I asked the Unseen One. "Did You want me to see these things so I could tell somebody about them?" I felt a surge of excitement go through me. Maybe the Unseen One wanted me to go back to my parents—to Odyssey —and tell them all that I'd seen here in Marus! "Is that what You want me to do?"

"Wait."

Startled, I looked around. Was somebody talking to me?

"Wait." It was a soft whisper that came from nowhere and everywhere at the same time.

I looked down at the man on the beach. He was sitting up now, looking around as if he were hearing the same thing as me.

"Wait."

"Is that You, Unseen One?" I asked. "Are You talking to me?"

"Waaay—aay—aay—"

The sound had direction now. It came from the path. I turned to look, curious and fearful about what I might see. A small lamb stumbled into the light.

I watched it suspiciously. Was it real? Did I mistake its bleating for the voice of the Unseen One? It gamboled toward me, stopped, looked me over, then sniffed its way into the cave. I followed it, still unsure whether it was real.

It stood next to the fire and bleated at me again.

I reached out and touched it. Its coat felt real and woolly and was a little damp from having been outside.

"Are you lost?" I asked the lamb.

It bleated in reply.

"You'd better stick with me," I told it. "You'll slip if you try to go back up the path, or you might fall off the cliff. Stay here where it's warm."

The lamb seemed to get my message. It went over to my

furry bed and lay down next to it. I went back out to the cliff, where the night was perfectly still. Down on the beach, Draven had gone. The fire was fading to a dull, red glow. I went back into the cave and crawled under the furs. The lamb sniffed at me, bleated one more time, then lowered its head and went to sleep.

A barking dog woke me the next morning. I lifted my head and rubbed my eyes. The lamb was also sitting up, its ears twitching at the sound.

Then came a voice. "Forma!" it called out.

The lamb stood up. So did I. Together we walked out onto the cliff and looked up the path. It was clear, but the dog was above, barking over the grassy edge. Then the face of a young man appeared.

He waved. "Hello!" he said.

"Hi," I replied, waving back.

"I think that's mine," he said, pointing at the lamb.

"I think you're right," I agreed. "I kept him in the cave with me through the night so he wouldn't get hurt."

"Thank you," the young man said gratefully. "He got separated from the rest of the flock. He often does. It seems like I'm always chasing him." He then called, "Come here, Forma, you naughty boy."

Forma stayed with me.

The young man put his hands on his hips. "Forma!"

The lamb didn't move.

"That's strange. He usually comes to me right away."

"I'll bring him up," I said and patted my leg at the lamb. "Come on, Forma."

I made my way up the path, with Forma following happily behind.

The young man was waiting at the top. The dog ran up to

sniff my trousers and hands. "You have a way with sheep," the man observed. "Are you a shepherd?"

"Who, me? No, I'm not," I replied. "But he seems friendly."

"I'm Watern, a shepherd for Legginth."

"Legginth?"

"He owns most of the land north of here."

"Nice to meet you."

Watern looked down the path. "I've been around here for years and never saw that path before. And you said there's a cave down there?"

"Uh-huh."

"Mind if I have a look?"

"It's not my cave," I explained. "I just stayed there last night because I didn't have anywhere else to go."

Watern went down the path and then returned a minute later. He looked at me with a strange expression on his face.

"What's wrong?" I asked.

"There's no cave down there."

I laughed. "Yes, there is."

But he was deadly earnest. "I promise, there's no cave."

Sure that he was pulling my leg, I went back down the path. The cliff seemed smaller than it had before—dangerously small, in fact. I couldn't have walked around it as I had last night. I turned to the cave and found myself face-to-face with a wall of rock.

"I don't believe it!" I exclaimed, pushing at the hard wall. "This is impossible!" I raced back up the path, stumbling as I went. "It was there!" I panted.

Watern spread his arms. "It's not there now."

At the top of the path, I tripped and Watern reached out to catch me. He gazed into my face, and we made full eye contact for the first time. "I understand now," he said simply.

"What do you understand?" I asked, getting more confused by the second.

He whistled for the dog, who was playfully chasing Forma around the field.

"What do you understand?" I asked again.

"Come home with me. Legginth will want to meet you." He strode off, with the dog joining him.

I followed along, wondering what I'd gotten myself into now. Forma ran up to my side and stayed close by like a friend.

The downs spilled into Legginth's private estate. The fields were fenced off and full of grazing cows and sheep. Legginth lived in a wide, one-story house that looked as if it had started off as a simple cottage and been added to over the years. Watern ducked inside, then came back a moment later with a short, rugged-faced man with long, dark hair and a matching beard.

"So you saved our Forma from disaster?" he called to me, his hand outstretched to be shaken.

I obliged. "I'm not sure," I said. "Forma might have saved *me*." Forma bumped against my leg as if he wanted my attention.

"He likes you," the man observed with a smile.

"I probably smell like a sheep," I joked.

The man was searching my face with his eyes. "Watern tells me you slept in a cave that mysteriously disappeared."

I nodded. "I can't figure it out." I wished he would quit looking at me like that.

"I might be of help," the man said. "My name is Legginth. I have taught your kind."

"My kind?"

"The chosen servants of the Unseen One."

"What do you mean? Why do you think I'm—"

Legginth laughed. "Come inside," he said and took my arm as if to guide me. The door we went through led to a kitchen. I could smell breakfast on the stove. A woman appeared from another door with eggs in her hand.

"Hello," she said and went to the stove. "I'm Minter."

"Hi. I'm Scott."

But that was as much as I got to say. Legginth continued to lead me through the kitchen, down a long, paneled hall, and straight into a bathroom.

"What's wrong?" I asked. I felt as if I'd been dragged to the principal's office.

On the wall was a mirror. He pointed at it.

"What's wrong?" I asked, looking at my reflection. I hadn't seen my face in a while and was surprised. I looked older. My hair had grown wild. But that wasn't what Legginth wanted me to see.

He pushed me closer. "Your eyes."

I looked—and then looked again. My eyes, which had always been brown, were now two different colors. One was green, and the other was blue. I stared at myself from this angle and then that angle. My mouth hung open in disbelief.

"What does it mean?" I wondered aloud.

Legginth tugged at my sleeve. "Come have breakfast. I want you to tell me your story."

And so, over eggs, bacon, toast, tomatoes, baked beans, and sausage, I told him everything that had happened to me. He and Minter, who turned out to be his wife, listened attentively and interrupted only to ask clarifying questions. I finished by saying, "So now I'm trying to find Draven."

Legginth leaned back, his fingers drumming lightly on the table. "You won't find him," he said confidently.

My heart sank. "I won't?" I protested. "But how will I—"

He held up a hand to stop me. "You won't find him. He will find *you*."

"How do you know that?"

Legginth and Minter exchanged glances. "You'll have to trust me. I know. You won't meet again until the Unseen One wants you to meet."

"What am I supposed to do in the meantime?"

Legginth stopped drumming his fingers. "You can stay here. If the rest of the sheep like you as much as Forma does, you can be one of my shepherds. Watern can teach you. And there are things I can teach you as well. Consider this your time of apprenticeship."

"Apprenticeship for what?" I asked.

Legginth smiled. "We'll discover that eventually, too."

Minter prepared a small room for me at the end of a ranch house where Watern and the rest of Legginth's workers lived. The room had a narrow bed, a dresser, and a washbasin. Then Watern introduced me to the rest of the workers. They were cordial enough. I was grateful that they didn't stare at my eyes. Watern must have warned them.

In a routine we would follow for the next few days, Watern took me out with him to shepherd the flocks. He taught me about their behavior, their habits, and the calls to use to make them do what I wanted. I learned that they were, for the most part, incredibly stupid animals. But they were gentle and affectionate to me. "They know a good shepherd when they see one," Watern said. He also drilled me on what to do if wolves, stray dogs, or bears attacked.

After a week, Watern made me take the sheep out by myself for the day. The following week, I led them to more-distant fields, where I actually spent the night with them under the open sky. And so it went for more than a month.

It was hard work, but I didn't mind. I liked the sheep and grew to love my time walking and thinking under beautiful blue skies or huddling under a tree when it rained. I found myself talking to the Unseen One more and more. I thought of my parents and wondered again if time were passing in Odyssey at the same pace as it was in Marus. I prayed that the Unseen One would somehow let them know I was all right. I remembered, too, what my parents had said to me about my being special—about how I had been a gift to them, which they knew they'd have to give back to God.

Legginth often called me to the main house in the evenings to talk about the history of Marus and the traditions of those who'd been chosen by the Unseen One. Legginth also gave me assignments to read from various history books about Marus. Then, one night, he brought out his own set of the Sacred Scrolls, which gave more-detailed accounts of the Unseen One's works.

I now learned the names of the kids who'd come from my world before. Each had been given a specific task to do, and then when it was done, had disappeared, presumably back to my world. I had hoped that I might recognize some of the names and imagined meeting them when I returned. But none of the names were familiar.

Legginth also gave me a notebook and pens. "Write down everything that's happened to you," he instructed. "Keep a chronicle of it all. Maybe the Unseen One will add it to the Sacred Scrolls."

I laughed at the idea that anything I'd written would be called sacred, but Legginth wasn't amused. I did what he asked.

One day during my second month with Legginth, when I was a full day's walk from Legginth's home, the sheep began to act very nervous. Starion, the sheepdog who often came with me, began to bark at a nearby grove of trees. I stood with a staff in hand, watching and smelling the air for any hint of what might be coming. A cold wind suddenly blew, and I felt a chill cover my body.

Suddenly, Draven stepped out of the woods and walked toward me. He looked older now, his hair longer and graying. But a fire burned in his eyes more vividly than ever before. I stood where I was and waited to see what he would say or do.

"You're cold," he said.

I was shivering now but didn't know what to say to him.

He took off his coat and draped it on my shoulders. "Come on, Scott," he urged gently. "The time has come. We have work to do."

"What about my sheep?" I asked.

"They're no longer your worry," he answered and looked beyond me.

I turned to look. Legginth stood on the crest of the hill with Watern, and they waved at me.

"Can I go and say good-bye?" I asked.

"Not now. You'll see them again."

I waved back. I was mystified by what was happening and suspected I might be having another dream. But Draven headed for the grove, and I followed.

"Where are we going?" I asked as we slipped into the shadows of the trees.

"We have unfinished business with Mobeck and Skalaw," he said firmly.

I drew his coat around me and stopped. "Wait a minute," I said, suddenly feeling ridiculous. "Hold on just a cotton-picking minute."

Draven stopped and turned to me. "What's wrong?"

"What's wrong?" I asked indignantly. "What's *wrong?* You ditched me with Gwynn and then disappeared for more than two months while I risked my life trying to find you, and then you suddenly show up and I'm supposed to follow you back where I might get killed by Mobeck and Skalaw?"

Draven put a finger to his chin for a moment, as if he had to think about it. "That's right," he finally said.

I shook my head. "Not so fast. I don't want to go anywhere until I understand a few things."

"What do you want to know?" he inquired, sighing impatiently.

"Well, for one thing, where have you been?"

"Not that I have to answer your questions, but I will because you are now a chronicler and need to write it down. When I ran from Deptford, I ran because I was scared. I thought Mobeck and Skalaw would come to their senses and turn to the Unseen One after time was restored. When they didn't, it frightened me. So I came to Eastcliff to hide. I was depressed and upset. I wanted to meet the Unseen One and tell Him my feelings. I wanted Him to know how alone I felt. I wanted to hear clearly from Him again before I did anything else in His name."

"And what happened?"

"I got my answer from Him on the beach."

"So it *was* you! You were kneeling next to a fire."

He nodded. "Did you witness the storm?"

"Yeah."

"And the tidal wave?"

"Yeah!" I said, excited to have the mystery solved. "Was that the Unseen One? Was He sending a message?"

"It was the Unseen One, but the message didn't come in the storm or the wave. It came after, in a voice as gentle as a lamb's fleece. It covered me and comforted me. It told me that I am not alone. Those who are still faithful and ready to serve

Him surround us. I also learned that you were to be trained, and then we would go back to face those who want us killed."

"But I still don't see how I fit into all this," I admitted.

"The Unseen One has chosen you to succeed me."

"Succeed you? You mean, I'm supposed to be your replacement?"

"Do you have a problem with that?"

"Well … no," I stammered. "I mean, I don't think so. But if I succeed you, what happens to you?"

"Leave that to the Unseen One."

"Okay. But what's going to happen to *me*? How long will I stay in Marus? I read about the others from my world and how they did their jobs and went home. When will I go home?"

"That's up to the Unseen One."

"But what about my parents?"

"They've been expecting this."

I thought of my dream about my parents in the cave. I thought of all the times they'd talked about my being special. "But I want to say good-bye to them," I protested. "Am I allowed to do that?"

"Have I ever chained you up or forced you to follow me?" He waved his hand ahead of us. Through the trees, I could see a house. It was *my* house!

I looked at Draven.

"Go on," he said.

I ran for it. I cleared the woods in seconds flat and raced across the lawn to the front porch. I took the steps two at a time and burst through the front door.

Everything seemed like a dream now. Maybe it *was* a dream. My mother and father were sitting in the living room. My father was reading a book, and my mother was doing the crossword puzzle in the newspaper. They looked up at me as I entered the room. I felt like a returning soldier who'd been away at war. My father slowly stood up, the book sliding from his lap to the floor, his face an expression of surprise. My mother gasped and threw herself on me. She pulled me close, hugging and kissing. Then I felt my father's arms around me, and the three of us stood in the living room and cried. I didn't know why they were crying. Maybe I'd been gone longer than I thought. But I cried, too—at the feel of them and the smell of my mother's perfume and my father's cologne.

All this happened without words. It was as if we couldn't speak. My mother and father stepped back from me, as if to look me over. With tears streaming down my face, I told them why I was there. "I came back to say good-bye," I explained at the end.

My mother held a tissue to her nose and dabbed her eyes. She nodded. My father reached out and patted my head the way he always did when he was proud of me but couldn't find the words to say. Like an electric current, an understanding passed between us. They *knew* a day like this would come. They *knew* I was going to be taken away. "To do something special," they'd always said. But now I realized those weren't just wishful thoughts or mere words on their part. They *knew* it would happen for real. And now it had.

I was still confused by their silence. Why didn't they speak?

"Can't you say anything to me?" I asked.

My mother checked her sobs long enough to say, "We love you."

My father forced a smile, then took off his glasses and wiped his eyes.

We hugged each other again, and I buried my face in their arms. I tried to lose myself in the darkness of that embrace.

"It's hard, I know," Draven said. I looked up. He was holding me close, patting me on the back. "All who are called are called to sacrifice. We must give up before we can take on."

We weren't in my home or even the woods anymore. The rumble beneath my feet and the noise of rushing wind told me we were in a train carriage. Thin lines of light came through the slats in the woodwork. The train whistle blew, and I could feel that we were slowing down.

"Hailsham?" I asked.

Draven nodded and pulled open the carriage door. It was daylight outside. "The Unseen One has a message for Mobeck and Skalaw," he said and leaped off the train.

CHAPTER FOURTEEN

W e journeyed from the Hailsham station across fields that were now familiar to me. We passed by the smaller village of Deptford and Gwynn's estate. The house had been rebuilt by Mobeck's soldiers and turned into a barracks. Rather than cut across the land, we followed the stone wall around to where it ultimately connected to Mobeck's private residence. There the wall had been knocked down. Construction was well under way for a large swimming pool and tennis courts.

"So they got what they wanted," I observed.

"They've got *more* than they wanted," Draven replied.

A guard stepped out from behind a tree. He pointed his rifle at us and threatened, "Don't move or I'll shoot."

"Put it away!" Draven snapped. "You're going to take us to the people we want to see anyway."

"I'm taking you to—" The guard stopped, realizing that Draven had already said what he was about to announce. "Oh. But don't try any tricks."

The guard marched us into the mansion. Other guards appeared, then retreated when they saw Draven.

"Where is Supreme Commander Mobeck?" the guard shouted at a nervous-looking servant.

"In the observation room," he replied, then ducked into a room.

We continued down the hall to a set of doors. The guard knocked loudly.

"What do you want?" Mobeck asked through a small intercom speaker on the wall.

"Vindall here, sir. I have Draven and his accomplice."

"You do?" the voice went up in pitch. "Where do you have them? In the prison?"

"No, sir. They are right here."

"Here? In my home? Did you catch them or did they come on their own?"

"They came on their own," the guard answered.

"By the two moons!" A buzzer sounded, and the two doors sprung open. The guard gestured for us to go in.

The room looked like a warehouse for an electronics store. Monitors were attached to the walls. Large gadgets with knobs and dials filled rows of tables. Some had speakers that buzzed, while others occasionally squealed. Mobeck appeared from behind a stack of machines that could have been computers.

"In a million years, I never thought you'd have the nerve to come back here," Mobeck said jovially. He'd obviously regained his confidence since I'd last seen him. "Would you like coffee or tea? I could also bring in some humble pie." He chuckled at his little joke, but he stopped when he saw the dark look Draven gave him. "What, no sense of humor? Never mind then. Why don't you come over here and look at these plans? I've annexed Gwynn's property next door and want to do some wonderful things with it."

Just then, Skalaw came through the door like a descending vulture. "So you came back!" she hissed. "I'm astounded. Guards! You know what to do with them!"

Several guards appeared in the doorway and trained their guns on us.

"Now, wait," Mobeck said to his wife. His voice had gained an edge to it. "He came all this way from wherever he was hiding. It must have been for a reason."

Skalaw turned on her husband. "You're too indulgent! If you were a real man, you'd have killed him ages ago and given me his teeth on a necklace."

Mobeck laughed nervously. "Perhaps for your next birthday."

Draven stood silently.

"By the two moons, it's awkward when you don't say anything!" Mobeck told him.

Skalaw chuckled. "Maybe he's afraid to speak. He might burst into tears and run away again."

I stepped forward to give them a piece of my mind, but Draven put his hand on my shoulder.

"Well?" Skalaw asked. "Don't waste any more of my time. Or do you run out of tricks when you don't have a big audience?"

Draven met their looks with a cold eye. Finally he declared, "The blood of Gwynn has cried out to the Unseen One."

Mobeck looked perplexed. "Gwynn? You came here to talk about Gwynn?"

"Your reign of lies and treachery is coming to an end." Draven pointed to one of the large television screens behind Mobeck. An image slowly appeared, blurry at first and then clearer as Draven spoke. "Where the blood of Gwynn was spilled, so will you fall."

The image filled the screen. Mobeck lay on the floor of the Hailsham city hall. He was dead—there was no mistaking it. He was surrounded by men who jeered and taunted his lifeless body. The image froze on the screen.

Draven continued, "Every man you considered a friend is becoming your enemy. You will be cut off from all you have trusted. The world will laugh when they remember the name of Mobeck."

Mobeck shoved his fist in his mouth and bit it, crying, "No!"

"Stop it! Stop it!" Skalaw commanded and slapped her husband.

Ignoring her, he cowered where he was, his eyes fixed on the image.

Draven pointed to a second monitor. "Skalaw, you have sold yourself and the people of Marus to pagan gods. The Unseen One has decreed your future."

"I won't look!" she shrieked. "I don't want to see!" But she couldn't resist it. She turned to see what was on the screen, and what she saw filled her with horror. Her dead body was being devoured in the streets of Sarum by vultures. "No!" she screamed and pointed accusingly at Draven. "You can't do this to me! I won't let you! Guards, take them away! I want them shot now! Do you hear me? Kill them now!"

But the guards stood still. They seemed mesmerized by the images on the screens.

"Somebody do something!" Skalaw cried out as she sank to her knees. She put her face in her hands and wept in loud, heaving sobs.

"Now you have seen the end," Draven told them. "But you don't know how or when it will come. Let that knowledge punish you until then."

Draven tipped his head toward the door for us to go. We walked toward the guards, and they cleared the way for us.

"Wait, Draven!" Mobeck shouted. He stumbled into the hall and fell at our feet. "Mercy! Have mercy on me! Tell me what to do and I'll do it! Please!"

Draven turned to him. "You know what to do. You have always known. But you've been too self-serving to do it." Then he strode down the hallway.

"Don't leave," Mobeck said tearfully, clutching at my leg. "Please."

I pulled away from Mobeck's reach and followed Draven out of the mansion.

I hadn't noticed before what a beautiful day it was. Birds were singing, and I could smell fresh-mown grass. It was an odd contrast to the oppression inside.

Draven took a deep breath. Without meaning to imitate him, I did the same. We looked at each other and smiled.

"It's not the last time we'll have to deal with them, is it?" I asked.

"Unfortunately, no," Draven answered. "But they won't be the same after today."

We headed back for Hailsham. Somewhere in the middle of a field, I stopped to look around. With a feeling of finality, I thought, *This is home now.*

The fields were green and stretched out to the village, while the land in the opposite direction was covered with woods. The sky was a rich blue. On the horizon, storm clouds gathered.

"Where are we going now?" I asked Draven.

"Wherever the Unseen One sends us," he replied.

We walked on. And then I realized I was still wearing his coat.

EPILOGUE

Jack, who'd been reading the pages after Whit, set the manuscript on the desk. He and Whit faced James, who sat on the
edge of his bed across the room.

"Questions?" he said.

"Where did it come from?" Jack asked.

He answered, "It was found by Mrs. McCutcheon in a stack
of homework she'd taken home to grade—nearly two weeks
after Scott disappeared."

"Then what happened?" asked Whit.

"She showed it to the police right away."

Jack chuckled. "I'm sure that went over well."

"They were patronizing," James said soberly. "They weren't
interested in a story in which Scott had disappeared to another
dimension. One detective had a theory that Scott had run away
and the story was his 'note' saying good-bye."

Whit raised his eyebrows. "The detective thought it was
written by Scott? They checked the handwriting?"

"Yes. But the police also begged Mrs. McCutcheon not to
show it to Scott's parents. They thought it would upset them
worse than they already were."

"What did Mrs. McCutcheon do?" Jack asked.

"She thought and prayed about it and then decided the police were wrong. She reasoned that Scott's parents were people of faith and might take comfort from the manuscript."

Jack sat up suddenly, like a schoolboy who'd figured out the answer to a question. "But Scott said in the story that he saw his parents. He talked to them. So they wouldn't need comfort from the manuscript."

"I'm coming to that," James replied. "Mrs. McCutcheon took the manuscript to Scott's parents. She told me later that they seemed to be acting strangely."

"Their son had been missing for two weeks. How else would they act?" Jack questioned.

James held up his hand and nodded. "That's what was so strange. They didn't act distraught or panicked. They were quiet and calm. They spoke like two people who were at peace."

"And then?"

"Mrs. McCutcheon told them about the manuscript. They looked it over and confirmed that Scott had written it. Mrs. McCutcheon assured them that she hadn't given Scott an assignment to write such a story, so she couldn't account for the story's existence. But Scott's parents didn't seem bothered by it at all. Finally Mrs. McCutcheon asked them directly why they were so at ease." James paused to drink some water.

"What did they say?"

James cleared his throat and continued. "Scott's parents explained that they had tried for years to have a baby but couldn't. Then, to their surprise, Scott came along. In their gratitude to God, they promised Scott to Him. So, from the beginning, Scott was consecrated to God. They always believed that God would take him away one day to use him in a remarkable way. But they never imagined it would be like that."

Jack leaned back in his chair and folded his arms. "Are you saying they accepted the story about Marus?"

James nodded. "Scott's parents confessed to having a dream a few days earlier. In their shared dream, Scott came to them and explained that he was doing God's work somewhere else. They didn't remember much else about it, except that it left them with a peace and comfort they had never experienced before. Mrs. McCutcheon left the manuscript with them, but not before making a copy."

"I wonder if we can talk to Scott's parents," Whit mused.

"You can try," James said. "But I spent years searching and couldn't find them. They left Odyssey a year or two after Scott disappeared, and no one around here knows where they are now. They might even be dead by now."

"That's a convenient dead end," Jack observed.

"It's not convenient for me," James countered. "I'd love for them to confirm the story. Scott was never found, you know.

His disappearance remains a mystery. The police ultimately gave up on the notion of foul play and concluded that Scott must have run away from home. There was no evidence to support their conclusion, of course. But that's how it ended."

Jack sighed heavily. "I don't know what to say."

"Say what you really think," James suggested.

"Then I'll be perfectly honest," Jack stated. "I'm skeptical. I started off wanting to believe it's all true. But I can't. There are too many unanswered questions. The biggest question being, do I believe that other worlds exist? And if so, does God do things there like He does here? It's too much to believe."

"What about you, Whit?" James asked.

Whit rubbed his eyes. "I can only say what I've said before. I enjoy exploring the possibilities and mysteries of God's creation. But I can't say I believe in these stories beyond a shadow of a doubt."

James seemed to deflate before their very eyes. He slumped down where he sat and stared at the floor.

"I hope you're not too disappointed," Whit said sympathetically.

"I had hoped the two of you might become the new keepers of the chronicles since I won't be around much longer," he replied.

"Why do you keep saying that?" Jack asked.

James looked up. "I am not a well man. My time is running

out. I thought you could be of help after you found the first manuscript. Obviously, I was wrong."

"I'd still like to see some of the other manuscripts," Whit said.

"What's the point? You admit you don't believe in them. And I'm not here to entertain you." James stood up. "Thank you for coming by, gentlemen."

Whit and Jack stood up, knowing they'd been dismissed. They lingered, each one wanting to say something to James that might encourage him. But there wasn't anything more to be said.

The two men left Hillingdale Haven.

"Is that the end of it?" Jack asked once they were in the car.

Whit looked at his friend and thought many different things. He said sadly, "I guess it is."

But it wasn't.

And now, a preview of the exciting *Passages*, Book 6!

CHAPTER ONE

"Look at that!" Michelle Brewer exclaimed from behind the bushes.

Danny Taylor grabbed her arm and pulled her down. "Get down!" he demanded. "Are you trying to get us in trouble?"

"Ouch!" Michelle said and rubbed her arm. "Don't ever lay a hand on me again, you male chauvinist!"

"What?" Danny asked, not sure what she'd said but suspecting from her tone that it wasn't nice.

"You heard me." She glared at him through her glasses.

Danny grunted and peered through the bush toward Trickle Lake. Though it was midafternoon on a hot summer's day, a bonfire raged along the shore. Dozens of teenagers—maybe even hundreds, Danny thought—were milling around the lake and in the nearby forest. Tents had been set up around the various campsites and picnic tables. Loud rock music blasted through a sound system that had been set up by the dock. A peculiar smell filled the air.

It was June 1968, and this was a music festival spontaneously arranged by a group from nearby Campbell Community College. Word had gone around to Odyssey's teens, and somehow Michelle had heard about it. Danny wasn't surprised. Michelle somehow heard about *everything*, whether she was supposed to or not.

The crowd of young people had started to gather at Trickle Lake around noon. Most of them were students, with long hair and Day-Glo headbands, psychedelic jewelry and tie-dye shirts, bell-bottoms and sandals, and peace signs and radical placards.

"I told you they were going to have a festival today," Michelle gloated. "Didn't I tell you?"

To be honest, Danny didn't much like Michelle. She was bossy and talked a lot and had to have everything her own way. She was the kind of girl who annoyed all the boys and got on the nerves of all the girls. Mostly her opinions got her into trouble. She always complained about how men were Neanderthals who oppressed women and said that one day women would rule the universe so they could truly be free. Danny figured Michelle expected to be the president when that happened.

So why was Danny with her now? He had no choice. Michelle was his cousin, and his parents expected him to be her friend when she came to visit, which she did every summer as soon as school was out.

Danny got the impression that Michelle was sent to them because everybody else was too preoccupied to deal with her. Michelle's mother was in Cleveland, busy running a political campaign for a seat in Congress. ("Summer is a hectic campaigning time," he'd heard her say.) And Michelle's father, who lived with his new wife in Seattle, was too busy with his new family. So it became Danny's chore to keep Michelle entertained and out of his parents' hair.

Today he had thought they were going to go play at McCalister Park, but then she had sprung this idea on him right after they had left the house.

"There's a big hippie festival up at Trickle Lake," she had said. "Wouldn't it be groovy to see it?"

"No," Danny had replied honestly.

"I want to see it!" Danny's younger brother, Wayne, had chimed in.

But Danny had snapped at Wayne to go home. It was bad

enough having to put up with Michelle. He didn't want his little brother tagging along, too.

Wayne had pouted and gone back to the porch.

Michelle had then ignored both Danny and Wayne, climbed on her bike, and taken off in the direction of Trickle Lake. Danny had leaped onto his bike and gone after her. The entire way up, he had argued with her until he was breathless. He had said they would get into trouble. He had said the students would yell at them for being there. It had been no use. He had thought about turning around and letting her go on her own, but he knew his parents would blame him if they got home from work and anything had happened to her.

"That's the life," Michelle said now, gesturing to the hippies from behind the bushes. "Freedom to do whatever you want, whenever you want. When women are in charge, this is how it'll be."

Danny wasn't impressed. It looked like nothing more than a big cookout. His family had them all the time, but without the long hair, loud music, and weird clothes.

A twig snapped behind them. Danny and Michelle spun around. Wayne stood there with an impish grin on his face.

"What are you doing here?" Danny cried out in a harsh whisper.

"Mom and Dad didn't want me to be home alone, remember?" Wayne responded, sounding like a smart aleck.

"You're 10 years old. You know how to be home alone."

"But Mom said—"

"Oh, be quiet and get down before somebody sees you!" Michelle snapped.

Wayne stooped down and crab-crawled over to them. "What's going on?" he asked as he tried to squeeze between them to see.

Danny frowned. "Nothing," he said disgustedly. "It's boring. Let's go home."

"Not yet," Michelle said. "You know what? I think it's safe."

"Safe? Safe to do what?" Danny asked.

Michelle started to crawl around the bush.

"What are you doing?" Danny asked, his voice rising in pitch.

"I want to mingle."

"Mingle! Are you nuts? They don't want some *girl* hanging around."

"They won't care. They're too laid-back to care." She came out from behind the bush and stood up, then took a scarf out of her back pocket and tied it around her mop of black hair. She adjusted her glasses on her freckled nose and stepped confidently toward the lake.

"I don't believe it!" Danny said with a groan.

Michelle wandered in and out of the clusters of students who were drinking out of cans or nibbling from bags of food they'd brought. No one seemed to notice her.

"She's right," Wayne said. "Nobody cares."

"That's only because it's so crowded."

"Then we can go look around, too," Wayne suggested. "It's going to get even more crowded pretty soon."

"No, we're staying—" Danny stopped in midsentence because something about what Wayne had just said caused him to think twice. "Wayne, what do you mean it's going to get more crowded?"

"Because of all the police cars."

"*What* police cars?" Danny asked, a sick feeling growing in his stomach.

"The ones I saw driving up when I was following you. They would have beat me here if I hadn't cut cross-country."

Danny grabbed his brother's shirt. "The police are coming? Why didn't you say something?"

Wayne shrugged. "I wanted to see them bust everybody."

"But if they bust everybody, they'll bust *us*, too!"

"Oh," Wayne said. "I didn't think of that."

Danny scrambled to his feet. "You stay here," he ordered. "I'll go get Michelle."

Feeling about as conspicuous as an elephant at a party of pink flamingoes, Danny made his way down to the small dock, which was the last place he'd seen Michelle. The music blasted through the speakers and pounded his head. A gruff voice sang about going on a magic carpet ride.

Danny felt a tug at his sleeve.

"You're going in the wrong direction," Wayne said and pointed. "She's over there."

"I told you to wait behind the bush!" Danny shouted at his brother.

"But you were going in the wrong direction," Wayne offered in his defense.

Danny pulled at his brother's arm. "Stay close to me."

No one seemed to notice them. The students had all gathered in small clusters, where they were chatting about things like the Vietnam War, a place called Berkeley, the Democratic Party convention in Chicago, and other things Danny didn't understand. A few sat around guitar players and smoked strange-looking cigarettes. Unlike Michelle, who talked constantly about what a great life she thought this was, Danny didn't like this party at all.

"Where is she?" he muttered irritably—and then walked right into her.

"Watch where you're going!" she shouted at him over the music. She adjusted her glasses and scarf and then fingered a necklace of beads.

Danny pointed at the necklace. "Where did you get that?" he asked loudly.

"That lady in the tent over there gave it to me." Michelle gestured broadly.

Danny glanced at the tent, where a young woman in a peasant dress and bright smile sat and offered homemade goods to whoever passed by.

"That's what I'd like to do," Michelle said into Danny's ear. "Be free all day and make things in a tent."

"Right now we have to get out of here!" Danny called over the blaring music. "The police are on their way!"

"What?" Michelle asked, tipping her ear toward Danny.

Danny spoke louder. "I said, the police are coming!"

A young man with a long mustache and granny glasses suddenly turned to Danny. "Did you say the cops are coming?" he asked.

"Yeah."

"I saw them first," Wayne added.

The young man turned quickly to the group he'd been talking to and yelled, "Cops!"

The word shot like cannon fire around that group and then to other groups, and suddenly there was a wild commotion as the students threw down their cigarettes and scrambled for the trees. A whistle blew from somewhere and then another from somewhere else, and the police swarmed in, their dark-blue uniforms a strange contrast to the surroundings. The music abruptly stopped, the sound replaced with shouts from the police and the students. An officer with a megaphone announced something about this being an illegal assembly and for everyone to stop where they were. No one did.

"My folks are gonna kill us! We've gotta get out of here!" Danny yelled. But there was nowhere to run. The police had moved in from all sides, and Danny, Michelle, and Wayne found themselves squeezed onto the small, wooden dock that reached out into the lake.

"The boats," Michelle said. There were small boats at the end of the dock, and she raced toward them. She seemed to think they could escape by paddling away. Confused about what to do, Danny and Wayne followed her. The three of them reached the ladder that led down to the boats. A crush of people, all with the same idea, arrived seconds behind them. Unfortunately, the back of the crowd didn't stop when the front of the crowd reached the end of the dock. Soon people were being pushed into the lake. Danny saw Michelle go head over heels into the water. In the next instant, he and Wayne were forced in, too.

Danny was a good swimmer and quickly pushed his way to the surface. He looked around for Wayne and Michelle but had a hard time seeing. Water was pouring down onto him from somewhere above, as if he'd come up under a waterfall. *But there's no waterfall at Trickle Lake*, he remembered, *so what's this falling on my head?* He kicked to get away from the annoying splashing but found that his feet touched bottom. He stopped, surprised. He knew for a fact that Trickle Lake was more than 10 feet deep here. Placing his feet firmly on the ground, he stood up. And up and up. And soon he found himself standing in knee-deep water.

He looked around. Michelle and Danny were also standing up, only a few feet away, with puzzled expressions on their faces. Danny couldn't believe his own eyes. They weren't standing in Trickle Lake anymore but in the center of a huge fountain in the middle of a large city center.